# SHARED PARENTING: Beyond the Great Divide

# SHARED PARENTING: BEYOND the GREAT DIVIDE

The Twenty Essential Co-parenting Tasks for Raising Children in Two Homes

## Frank Leek, PhD

iUniverse, Inc.
Bloomington

**Shared Parenting: Beyond the Great Divide**
**The Twenty Essential Co-parenting Tasks for**
**Raising Children in Two Homes**

iUniverse books may be ordered through booksellers or by contacting:

iUniverse
1663 Liberty Drive
Bloomington, IN 47403
www.iuniverse.com
1-800-Authors (1-800-288-4677)

Because of the dynamic nature of the Internet, any web addresses or links contained in this book may have changed since publication and may no longer be valid. The views expressed in this work are solely those of the author and do not necessarily reflect the views of the publisher, and the publisher hereby disclaims any responsibility for them.

Any people depicted in stock imagery provided by Thinkstock are models, and such images are being used for illustrative purposes only.

Certain stock imagery © Thinkstock.

ISBN: 978-1-4759-2278-3 (sc)
ISBN: 978-1-4759-2280-6 (hc)
ISBN: 978-1-4759-2279-0 (e)

Library of Congress Control Number: 2012908415

Printed in the United States of America

iUniverse rev. date: 06/21/2012

# Contents

# Acknowledgments

Several people have helped me put down on paper my ideas about effective shared parenting: Carol Greenfield; Bill Leek; Jane Leek; Don Goering; Jean Goering; Joel Leek; Lisa Newell; Bud Brown; Lavonda Brown; Bob Adelstein; Carole Adelstein; Ede Leek; Kim Ferguson (and the epic five, who are also awesome: Katelyn Ferguson, Hailey Ferguson, Tom Ferguson, Sam Lowen, and Annie Claire Lowen); Eric Lowen; Lynn Ferguson; Mort Rumberg; Susan Rumberg; Mitch Cohen; Mary Lou Anderson; Lori Fortenberry; Keith Fortenberry; Eric Wright and Beatrice Wright, whom I forgot to thank; judges Patrick, Ridgeway, Kobayashi, and McBrien; the hundreds of therapists who have attended one of my workshops about the Shared Parenting Support Program; and finally, Celti and Wheati, who have accepted my writing efforts without question.

# INTRODUCTION

## What to Do When Hell Freezes Over

The judge gently tapped her gavel, ending the six-year marriage between Aaron and Nancy. Their divorce was final, at least legally. They had been divorcing for more than two years, and their anger had increased over that time. The judge admonished them to cooperate in the best interest of their child. Her final order was for Aaron and Nancy to share custody of their daughter Aria, switching every other week, and to enroll in counseling to learn co-parenting skills. Nancy was willing to start counseling, but Aaron was not. He was still emotionally bruised by the divorce process and was reluctant to begin therapy, saying, "I will sit down in the same room with that woman when hell freezes over!"

Several months later, Aaron called his attorney and said, "Well, I guess hell just froze over." The attorney referred Aaron and Nancy to a therapist who had worked with many two-home families, using the Shared Parenting Support Program. During the intake session, Aaron said their daughter had recently spilled a glass of milk and become very agitated about it. She looked up at him and said, "I try to be good, Daddy; don't leave!" He realized that the residue of marital conflict was not just between the parents; it affected their child as well.

## Moving from the Conflicts of Divorce to the Conflicts of Shared Parenting

After the divorce is finalized, mediators, attorneys, evaluators, and judges move on to other families, leaving the divorced parents with the most difficult task of all: moving past their own conflicts and learning to raise their child in two homes.

When parents separate, they vow their child will not be hurt, believing their child will actually be better off living in two homes, sheltered from the arguments of two unhappy, bickering parents. As they go through the divorce, parents find it difficult to remain focused on the goal of keeping the child out of the conflict. When they realize that their child is hurting, they accept that they must learn new skills, working together to help their child adjust to the many changes brought about by divorce. As uncomfortable as it might feel, they must talk with each other, for the sake of their child.

After the separation and divorce, most parents begin to rebuild their lives, working to avoid prolonged conflict and making sure their child is cared for. But learning to raise a child in two homes is not easy. Anger between divorcing parents endures. They are angry, not because they are bad or mean, but because they are stuck. And they are stuck because they haven't learned the new boundaries. In fact, most of the parents who continue to fight do so only because they don't know how to stop. Once parents learn the basic skills of shared parenting, they can move past their conflict and get down to the business of raising their child in two homes. As they learn co-parenting skills, the goal is not to become good friends. Rather, it is to develop a new relationship based on respectful boundaries. As a parent striving to raise a child in two homes, you can be in a crisis mode for only so long before something has to give. You can develop terrible headaches. You can go broke. You can become cranky and irritable. You can give up all the joys of life and focus only on how weak and helpless you are in the face of the other parent's terrible, controlling behavior. Or you can move from the crisis of divorce conflict to the lifelong practice of shared parenting. If you do that, you will have time to develop a hobby, go back to school, get a new career, or even make new friends.

## About This Book

This book is based on the Shared Parenting Support Program (SPSP), a co-parenting therapy that has been in use for more than twenty years. The parents and stepparents meet with an SPSP therapist weekly, following a highly structured program in a safe environment to learn how to put aside their conflicts and move on with their lives.

The purpose of *Shared Parenting: Beyond the Great Divide* is to help you along the path of recovery and discovery. Recovery from divorce, if you let it, can be a growth experience, or you can hold on to anger, resentment, and rage, forever remaining a victim. Discovery can be the process of growth and change for the good of all.

Parents choose to raise their children in two homes for varying reasons. Some parents have never lived together, and their relationship consisted of a single sexual contact. Some parents lived together and never married. Some parents married, had children, and then decided to live separately, resulting in a two-home family. Although each reason reflects a difference in emotional attachment, this guide applies to all reasons.

Shared parenting does not necessarily mean "fifty-fifty." As long as there are two parents, each without a fatal flaw that creates a danger to the child, they are faced with the tasks of sharing parenthood. Whether the ratio is fifty-fifty or one to ninety-nine, each child deserves the best of each parent, which can be achieved only by parent-to-parent communication and a modicum of parental maturity.

As you read this book, you will learn a method of co-parenting a child who is living in two homes. The method is based on several sources: my experience of working with families over the past sixty years; my colleagues who have completed the SPSP workshop for professionals and subsequently assisted families in improving their shared-parenting skills; and most importantly, the many parents I have met over the years as they've worked hard to create a positive life for their children.

An important source of information has been the workshops I have attended over the past twenty years, conducted by the leaders in understanding and helping the families of divorce. Those leaders of the field include Isolina Ricci, Richard Emory, Joan Kelly, Judith Wallerstein, and Mavis Heatherington. Twenty years ago, when I first focused on divorce issues, there was very little written about the subject. Now there are thousands of articles, journals, and books. I have contributed a few journal articles myself. The Internet, of course, is replete with information about divorce issues. As with all material on the subject, read carefully, and draw your own conclusions.

My goal is to present one way of meeting the challenges of raising children in two homes. I would encourage each parent to draw their own conclusions, use what works for them, and use their own knowledge, emotions, and resources to move past this difficult patch in life.

## Caveats

The information, ideas, and suggestions in this book are not intended as a substitute for professional advice. Before following any suggestions contained in this book, you should consult your personal physician or mental-health professional. Neither the author nor the publisher shall be liable or responsible for any loss or damage arising as a consequence of your use or application of any information or suggestions in this book.

Also, the information, ideas, and suggestions in this book are not intended to render legal advice. Before following any suggestions contained in this book, you should consult your personal attorney. Neither the author nor the publisher shall be liable or responsible for any loss or damage allegedly arising as a consequence of your use or application of any information or suggestions in this book.

## Examining the Possibility of Gender Bias

Several colleagues have noted that more than half of the vignettes show a bias toward mothers, showing them to be problematic and the fathers as victims. I can only plead the luck of the draw. I flipped a coin to determine who would be the problematic person. So hopefully it is a matter of chance and not an underlying bias on my part.

**Assessing Your Skills as a Co-parent, Now and Later**

Some parents like to use checklists to keep track of their progress as co-parents. You can use the assessment of co-parenting skills either as divorced parents working together or on your own. If you wish, make extra copies of this assessment so that you can go back later and review your progress.

1.  ACCEPTING PERSONAL RESPONSIBILITY

We no longer place all the blame on the other parent and have now reached the point of understanding that each is now responsible for our own shared-parenting skills.

Cannot do at all    1    2    3    4    5    Perform easily  _____

We no longer seek the approval of the other parent, realizing that the need for such approval is a carryover from our previous relationship. We now understand that we each must act independently, yet still work together in the best interest of our child.

Cannot do at all    1    2    3    4    5    Perform easily  _____

2.  MAINTAINING BOUNDARIES BETWEEN OUR HOMES

We have reached the point of being able to act independently, keeping each other informed of our thoughts, plans, and actions regarding our child, but not forced to give details of our everyday life.

Cannot do at all    1    2    3    4    5    Perform easily  _____

We understand and agree that as co-parents we must communicate between ourselves and not pass messages through our child.

Cannot do at all    1    2    3    4    5    Perform easily  _____

We understand that arguing has nothing to do with problem solving. We have moved past arguing, realizing that to argue is self-indulgent and harmful to our child.

Cannot do at all　1　2　3　4　5　Perform easily　_____

We understand that we must learn new decision-making skills. If we hold different opinions about how best to meet the needs of our child, we will first discuss the issue between ourselves. If we are unable to come to a decision, we will meet with a mediator so that a decision can be appropriately reached.

Cannot do at all　1　2　3　4　5　Perform easily　_____

## 3. EFFECTIVE PARENT-TO-PARENT COMMUNICATION

We have developed a no-fault, nondefensive way of communicating urgent messages regarding our child's daily needs.

Cannot do at all　1　2　3　4　5　Perform easily　_____

We have developed a system of regular parent-to-parent phone calls to share ongoing information regarding our child in a business-like manner.

Cannot do at all　1　2　3　4　5　Perform easily　_____

We have developed a system of communication about the long-range needs of our child.

Cannot do at all　1　2　3　4　5　Perform easily　_____

## 4. SUPPORTING THE OTHER PARENT'S POSITIVE TRAITS

We want our child to have the best of both parents, and we support each other's positive traits in the eyes of our child.

Cannot do at all   1   2   3   4   5   Perform easily   _____

## 5. DEVELOPING A POWERFUL CO-PARENTING TEAM

We understand that the co-parenting team consists of parents and stepparents. We are developing ways to use the skills and abilities of all team members to enhance the life of our child.

Cannot do at all   1   2   3   4   5   Perform easily   _____

We understand that if the co-parenting team is in conflict, our child will suffer, and when the co-parenting team is working cooperatively, the combined skills can enhance our child's life.

Cannot do at all   1   2   3   4   5   Perform easily   _____

## 6. PROVIDING EASY ACCESS TO EACH PARENT

We have the ability to allow our child easy access to each parent.

Cannot do at all   1   2   3   4   5   Perform easily   _____

## 7. DEVELOPING AN EFFECTIVE, PUBLIC CO-PARENTING TEAM

We understand that co-parenting should be invisible to teachers, scout leaders, and other persons who have frequent contact with our child, that we should not air our problems in public.

Cannot do at all   1   2   3   4   5   Perform easily   _____

We have learned to play zone defense when we meet in public, permitting easy, conflict-free interchange between parent and child.

Cannot do at all    1    2    3    4    5    Perform easily    _____

We have learned that our child is sensitive to our conflicts and is easily embarrassed if we argue in public.

Cannot do at all    1    2    3    4    5    Perform easily    _____

## 8.   MONITORING OUR CHILD'S WELFARE

We have learned that we must, in a no-fault manner, communicate regarding our child's welfare, sharing both positive and negative information.

Cannot do at all    1    2    3    4    5    Perform easily    _____

## 9.   AVOIDING POWER STRUGGLES

We know it takes two to have a power struggle. When we engage in a win/lose argument, our child always loses.

Cannot do at all    1    2    3    4    5    Perform easily    _____

We understand that when a marital relationship ends, only the impasse issues remain. As effective co-parents, when we are faced with an impasse issue, we move on without becoming embroiled in bitter conflict.

Cannot do at all    1    2    3    4    5    Perform easily    _____

## 10. MOVING ON, EMOTIONALLY AND PHYSICALLY

We have moved from the crisis of divorce to the understanding that although we have chosen not to live together, we will share the task of raising our child in a responsible, mature manner.

Cannot do at all      1    2    3    4    5      Perform easily      _____

We understand that we have physically separated and that the process of emotional separation will take time. We respect each other's independence and understand that our only connection is our child, whom we agree to raise to be a happy, self-assured, responsible adult.

Cannot do at all      1    2    3    4    5      Perform easily      _____

## Go to Great Lengths to Avoid Extremes

I want to point out two basic facts: First, no one is perfect. So if you gave yourself all fives and the other parent all ones, go back and at least acknowledge some imperfection. People will like you better for doing so. Second, no one is a total failure. If you gave yourself all ones, go back and give yourself a couple of threes and maybe a five. Doesn't that feel better?

# PART 1

------ ◆◆◆ ------

# The Transition

Making major life decisions involves both intellectual and emotional issues. Part 1 focuses on the intellectual decisions that you will be faced with as you make these major life decisions.

# CHAPTER 1

## Staying Together or Divorcing

The transition begins when one or both parents make the decision to separate. Even if you have made that decision, read this chapter and take a few minutes to reflect on your decision. The more thought you give to this important decision, the fewer regrets you will later have. If you have decided to remain together, seek the best help and support you can. If you have chosen to separate, make sure your reasons are well thought out and then move on. If you have decided to raise your child in two homes, the rest of the book is for you.

The transition continues with physically separating, filing for divorce, establishing two homes, taking care of yourself, and explaining to your child what is happening. During the transition, you will learn about the dissolution process, the costs, the terms, and the use of declarations and depositions, as well as the processes of mediation and evaluation. You will know the transition period is coming to an end when a court order is in place, the decree is final, and you have a court document outlining the division of property, what support is to be paid, and a parenting plan for your child.

You shouldn't get married just because you are standing in front of your friends, facing a member of the clergy who is about to ask a question that usually is answered with "I do." Nor should you get a divorce just because you have filed papers with the court to do so. Although the purpose of this book is to help you and the other parent learn to co-parent successfully after separation and divorce, first consider the possibility of staying together.

### Three Common Reasons for Divorce

Common reasons for divorce are destructive behavior, character differences, and the normal stress of marriage, discussed in detail here.

## Destructive Behavior

Divorce is an option when a parent is acting in a way that endangers one or both parents and/or the child. Dangerous behaviors include physical violence, emotional abuse, drug and alcohol abuse, criminal acts, chronic poor judgment, untreated emotional conditions, and a persistent failure to maintain a committed relationship. If the destructive behavior threatens injury or death, move to safety. If the other parent is potentially physically or emotionally abusive, you have the responsibility of placing very clear limits and not accepting behavior that exceeds those limits. You can then examine your part in the abuse, whether it is goading the other parent into such acts; tolerating such acts; believing that life offers no respite; or, having grown up in an abusive environment, believing such behavior is "normal." Clearly state your boundaries and limits and the consequences if the threat of abuse continues or escalates. Become involved in an anger management program, co-dependency treatment, and couples counseling. The final step, if changes are not made, is separation.

*Visiting Jail as a Life Occupation*

If the other parent can't seem to stay out of jail, it is generally best to divorce and work toward personal growth. Try not to think of yourself as someone who associates with a person who acts in ways that lead to being jailed. Only you can say when enough is enough. Counseling may be required to determine why you have agreed to such a lifestyle for yourself and your child.

## Unfaithfulness Hurts, but Is It Fatal?

If the other parent chooses to not be loyal to the marriage, you have a choice: either work very hard in treatment to determine what happened and rebuild a very injured relationship, or leave. If you decide to stay and it happens again, realize that your partner is not committed to a monogamous relationship and decide whether that behavior is tolerable to you.

When parents are in the process of separation and still want to work on their relationship, it is imperative that both agree not to have an intimate relationship with another person during the time of recovery.

## When Drugs Are More Important Than You or Your Child

If the other parent uses alcohol or drugs to the point it interferes with everyday life and he or she refuses to get help or quit, you have little choice but to leave the relationship and protect your child and yourself. Criminals and addicts are very adept at saying they are sorry, promising never to be bad again. Do not believe these words. Believe only actions. A person with a drug problem has a very difficult task: to prove that he or she is no longer drinking, using drugs, or breaking the law. It is that person's job to earn your trust, not yours to give trust without proof.

You can be a model citizen all your life, but rob just one bank, and you are a bank robber forever. Don't feel sorry for the bad guy. Robbing a bank is not like spilling milk. Saying "oops!" just isn't enough. When you are convinced the other person has reformed, using whatever measure you want, then you can consider starting the relationship again. No one knows how long it takes to reform. Six months is not enough. Bad guys say they can hold their breath longer than that.

## Untreated Emotional Conditions

When the other parent has an untreated emotional problem, such as schizophrenia, a bipolar disorder, or an obsessive-compulsive disorder, you can easily be caught in a bind. It is true that these conditions are based on stress and biology. Treatment and medications are needed to help the person gain control of the symptoms that are harmful to self and others.

We humans are a compassionate group and do not toss out persons with a broken leg, a brain tumor, or an emotional condition. We seek to support and help as best we can.

But what if a person refuses to obtain the needed treatment? Some of the medications have uncomfortable side effects. It is the work of the physician and the patient to overcome resistance to treatment. But what if the person refuses to get help? You are then faced with a major decision. Should you continue to protect the person because of the disorder or separate from the person for refusing to get better? That is when you consider your own endurance and your own safety. That is when you strongly consider the well-being and safety of your child.

## Character Differences

The second major reason for divorce is that the character of each parent is very different, and neither is willing to tolerate the other. Major problems can occur when the relationship is based on maladaptive behavior that developed early in life. Some people advocate marrying an opposite because it is more exciting. Some people say we marry opposites to work through differences. Research says if you marry someone with your same history and values, the relationship is more likely to endure.

There are some classical differences with which couples struggle. Some of these basic personality differences are listed here. As I have tried to emphasize, no one is all bad, and no one is all good. If you wish, rate yourself and the other parent on each of these character traits, placing an X where you are on the continuum and an O where the other parent is on the same scale. For example, let's say you are a neat freak, and the other parent has been known to leave shoes in the front room unattended. You might rate the neat/sloppy traits as:

Neat      X      2      3      4      O      Sloppy

So rate each of you on these character traits.

| | | | | | | |
|---|---|---|---|---|---|---|
| Neat | 1 | 2 | 3 | 4 | 5 | Sloppy |
| Fast | 1 | 2 | 3 | 4 | 5 | Slow |
| On time | 1 | 2 | 3 | 4 | 5 | Late |
| Humorous | 1 | 2 | 3 | 4 | 5 | Serious |
| Needy | 1 | 2 | 3 | 4 | 5 | Care-taking |
| Vulnerable | 1 | 2 | 3 | 4 | 5 | Protective |
| Sociable | 1 | 2 | 3 | 4 | 5 | Reclusive |
| Accepting | 1 | 2 | 3 | 4 | 5 | Demanding |
| Affectionate | 1 | 2 | 3 | 4 | 5 | Cool |
| Takes chances | 1 | 2 | 3 | 4 | 5 | Plays it safe |
| Honest | 1 | 2 | 3 | 4 | 5 | Dishonest |
| Controlling | 1 | 2 | 3 | 4 | 5 | Submissive |

When a couple first get together, the personality differences are often seen as humorous, exciting, and attractive. However, after the marriage settles into a routine, those same differences can become sources of annoyance. Mom may have been attracted to Dad's decisive, no-nonsense, take-charge personality. Three years and one child later, she views him as a Napoleonic dictator or worse. Dad may have been attracted to Mom's casual, fanciful ways. Now he views her as flighty and irresponsible.

Very tolerant people are able to make an opposite relationship work, but it is very difficult. It requires hard work to channel each parent's unique way of viewing the world, to tone down excesses, and to be tolerant of differences. Most often, each parent demands that the other parent change, believing that such changes would permit them to live together in harmony. That is not true. The way for opposites to get along is for each one to accept the behavior of the other and tolerate the differences. That is not easy to do.

*Surviving Character Differences*

- Neither you nor your partner can make basic personality changes. Most of your ways of seeing the world are hardwired into your personality by the time you are five. Just ask any kindergarten teacher.
- Each of you can tone down your individuality, but your basic personality traits will remain.
- Individual therapy will help you modify your own personality.
- The key to getting along with an opposite personality is to accept the differences.
- By working together, you can make compromises that will help you get along.
- Couples therapy will help you compromise and accept differences.
- The person asking for change is the one who must change.
- Read the preceding point again.

## The Normal Stress of Marriage

Sometimes living in a committed relationship is hard work and no fun. It is normal in a relationship to become so conflicted and frustrated that separation seems the only way out of despair. When the crisis passes, the couple can stay together, mature, and be better individuals, partners, and parents.

A "normal" relationship is one in which partners share similar but not identical views and have similar but not identical personalities.

Problems faced may include unevenness of maturity, imbalance of power, unmet needs for care and affection, failure to have family goals, and the changing character of love over time in a committed relationship. This group of parents represents the greatest increase in divorce over the past fifty years. As divorce has become easier, parents have viewed it as a more readily available way of leaving a frustrating situation. It makes a lot of sense to divorce if one parent is destructive, and it can be understood if parents have opposite personalities and have no way to accept each other's behavior. Parents in this third group, who are going through the normal ups and downs of married life, represent the casualties of no-fault divorce. No-fault divorces have resulted in many parents prematurely abandoning the ship of matrimony.

*Surviving Bad Times in a Good Relationship*

There are three things you can do to determine whether the relationship can be maintained.

1. Give it time. All relationships have ups and downs. Stay in the relationship unless there is danger, even if you are frustrated, to determine whether you can work together to make changes.
2. Use resources, such as growth seminars, family, friends, counseling, and church, to address the differences.
3. Maintain emotional balance. Do not use destructive means such as an affair, drugs, or violence to gain distance.

## The Benefits of Marriage

Marriage is a big-time business. A couple remaining together twenty-five years with an income of $40,000 a year will have managed a million dollars together. Even with more limited income, the family as a corporation can manage a "good life." The first step is to determine what your corporation wishes to accomplish. What are the goals to which you as a couple might aspire? Following are some of the goals you can pursue, which can be accomplished only by working together, having a vision for the future, and knowing how to manage resources to make the vision real.

## Having a Trustworthy, Loyal Companion

By vowing to be together through good and bad times, sickness and health, partners are agreeing that they have such a bond; thus, each person can be assured of loyalty and trust. In no other place in a person's life does this promise exist. When you go to work for a corporation, you do not take a vow that you will remain together in sickness and in health, for good and for bad. You know that you have certain rights but can be laid off if the company falters. You can be fired if you don't perform well or do something wrong. You can quit if a better job comes along. A marriage relationship is more enduring and includes fidelity and watching your partner's back.

## Sharing the Enjoyments and Vicissitudes of Life

Life is not an escalator that moves unerringly toward happiness. Part of being a family is having a history of life's good times and bad times. Without the emotional ties of a family unit, your history would be very boring.

## Having an Active Sex Life

There are two main purposes of sex: pleasure and reproduction. They are not mutually exclusive. In many marriages, sex becomes confused with power. When a couple can preserve a playful, friendly togetherness without fear or loathing, they will live longer and be happier. One client lamented, "We don't have as much floor play as we used to." Remember that there are eighteen thousand positions, half of which require floor play.

## Raising Children to Be Good Citizens

One of the main functions of many families is to have children and effectively socialize them to become responsible, productive citizens. Common methods, common values, and consistency accomplish this. A child has a basic need to be secure, cared for, and given positive direction. The family is the crucible of this goal.

## Joint Decision Making

It is helpful for parents to developed a decision-making style that permits both partners to contribute to the direction of the marriage: what sources of income, where to live, what type of residence, how to raise children, and how to spend spare time. Although most marriages do well without a master plan, partners can and do work together to organize the resources of the family for the good of all. Decision making must be mutual and not ruled by fear or manipulation.

## The Benefits of Divorce

It is easy to focus on the bad parts of a marriage and the reasons for leaving the failed relationship. Look at the benefits of divorce as well.

### Protection

Divorce is often the best way to get out of a destructive relationship. There are some people who, for whatever reason, are unable to follow the rules of society and represent a danger to others. In a marriage, such a person represents a physical and emotional danger to you as well as your child. By leaving such a relationship, you can protect yourself and your child.

### Personal Growth

If you find yourself drawn to potential partners whose values and beliefs are greatly different from your own, you will need to do some work before becoming involved with someone else. Honestly ask yourself why you have made such choices in the first place. There are many organizations and groups that can help you understand your motivation. If you are willing to learn from your mistakes, you can move on, making better choices in your life. The opportunity for personal growth is there.

### Safety and Growth of Your Child

If you are in a truly destructive relationship, your child will suffer as well. You must be very sure that your partner has a destructive personality to the point where a judge will agree you should be the sole decision-maker for your child. You may become convinced the other parent is destructive only to find that the court grants that person ongoing and frequent contact with your child. That parent will continue to be involved in your life and the life of yur child, and you will have even less control than you did before.

### Caution

Parents should be aware that learning to co-parent is often more difficult than saving a marriage. Divorce does not solve problems; it merely changes them. When you reach the point of despair and decide to separate, you likely will do so believing that the future will bring about a better, more

21

fulfilling life with positive and loving relationships. Unfortunately, this is at times untrue. The pressures of divorce and co-parenting often exceed the pressures of even a poorly functioning but intact relationship. If you had difficulty making parental decisions when you were together, making co-parenting decisions is even more difficult. When you divorce, you are faced with the challenge of learning to co-parent with someone you have chosen to no longer live with. Amid the anger of separation, you and the other parent must learn to make plans for and to care for your child.

## A Worksheet for Making Your Own Decision

Making a decision to stay in or get out of a relationship is very difficult. Some people prefer to think through the issues alone. Others prefer to discuss the issues with someone else. Both methods are effective, each reflecting a personality type. For those of you who make decisions only by talking to others, take some time to be alone and reflect. For those of you who go inside yourself to make decisions, go public and discuss your plans with someone else. The following questions are those I have heard most often from parents who are thinking about separating. You can use this as a workbook, but also seek advice from friends, relatives, religious mentors, and marriage therapists. When you are going through the process of making this decision, minimize your bad habits as much as possible. Don't give in to your addictions. Complete this process with as clear a mind as possible. Otherwise, your bad habits will keep you from being realistic about yourself.

When you have a couple of hours with no distractions, think about these questions. Use your common sense, your moral sense, and your parenting sense.

## Thinking about Your Decision

- What were the three main traits you saw in your partner that made you decide to make a lifelong commitment?
- What are the three main traits you now see in your partner that most make you want to separate and divorce?
- What were the three main traits your partner saw in you that made him or her decide to make a lifelong commitment?

- What are the three main traits your partner sees in you that make him or her want to separate or divorce?
- What is the single strongest reason to stay married?
- What is the single strongest reason to divorce?
- How will separation affect you, the other parent, your friends, your parents, and your in-laws?
- What is the worst outcome of separation?
- What is the best outcome of separation?
- What is the worst outcome of staying together?
- What is the best outcome of staying together?
- What aspects of your partner's behavior must change if you are to remain married?
- What major aspects of your behavior must you change if you are to remain married?
- List all the things you alone must do if you decide to stay together.
- List all the things you must do if you decide to separate and divorce.
- Write a marriage contract that will help you and your spouse lead a more positive life.
- Write a financial divorce contract.
- Write a parenting responsibility plan, outlining in detail when your children will be with each parent after separation.

## You Decide

Making the decision is something only you can do. Over the past fifty years, the mood of society has been to make divorce easier, to say it is without fault. Yet everyone I know who has divorced feels guilty and blames the other parent. In fact, the more guilty they feel, the more they blame the other parent. Make your decision based on information and clear thinking. If you decide to stay in the relationship, then work hard to learn how to develop a more mature relationship that will bring satisfaction to both parents and to your child as well.

If you decide to move on, then the rest of the book is a system of meeting the many challenges of raising your child in two homes.

# CHAPTER 2

--------◆-◆-◆--------

# Good Attorneys, Bad Attorneys,
# and No Attorneys at All

Your first decision will be whether to act as your own attorney or hire an attorney. More and more parents are choosing to act as their own attorney. If you are analytical and objective, and have writing skills, you may want to act as your own attorney. Courts are now providing assistance to parents who are able to put aside their conflict, divide the family assets, and develop a positive parenting plan. If you begin to feel lost, or if the other parent hires an attorney, then you should do so as well. It has been my observation that an attorney is a necessity. Acting as your own attorney makes you very vulnerable.

All attorneys must advocate for their client. Whether that is a positive or negative is for you to decide. An attorney will hear only your side of the story and will be prepared to argue your case in court. That is good. However, some attorneys will, without hearing the other parent's side of the story, become overly supportive of defending your version of the truth, and that can be bad. There is rarely one parent who is totally right and another who is totally wrong.

## Interviewing Attorneys

If you decide to hire an attorney, select one who specializes in family law. Interview prospective attorneys. Determine if your personalities match. If you are a quiet, easygoing person, avoid attorneys who want to "fight," "win," "pay back," and "get even." Be cautious if an attorney talks about "winning." The attorney may view children as objects, prizes to be won in court. Many attorneys will grant you a brief interview to get acquainted and provide some information about the procedures. Take advantage of this when you can.

## Questions to Ask When Interviewing Attorneys

- Are you a certified family law specialist?
- How long, on average, does it take to get a divorce?
- How do you work to reduce the conflict?
- What do you do if your client tells you to "get" the other partner?
- How much, on average, does it cost to get a divorce?
- How many divorces have you done?
- What order of intervention do you prefer?

## Attorney for Your Child

If the process of divorce becomes very conflicted and protracted, and a child is caught in the middle of the legal battle, it is sometimes a good idea to ask the court to appoint an attorney for the child. This is a very specialized area, and the attorney must be selected very carefully. The attorney must be able to understand the child's best interest as well as what the child wants. For example, a child may be enthralled with spending time with Dad, who has little structure and is far too lenient. The child may report to the attorney a preference to be with Dad, rather than with Mom, who has a positive structure. The attorney must be aware that what a child wants is sometimes not what a child needs.

## Jokes to the Contrary

It has been my experience that attorneys come in various sizes and belief systems. Most, in my experience, although charged with the responsibility of advocating solely for their client, have been compassionate and responsible, understanding the needs of families in conflict.

# CHAPTER 3

---

# Selecting a Mental-Health
# Professional without Going Crazy

When selecting a mental-health professional to help you develop a parenting plan for your child, you will find that there are psychologists, psychiatrists, social workers, and marriage therapists, all referred to as mental-health professionals. Following is an overview of some of the services you can expect from a mental-health professional who has specialized in working with parents who are now raising or are contemplating raising their child in two homes.

## Separation Consultant

Parents preparing to possibly divorce may seek the help of a mental-health professional to ensure that their child will be protected during the divorce process. The client in this situation is the child as represented by the parents. The parents relate where they are in the process of separation. The therapist helps them understand the developmental needs of their child and provides information about the effects of parental separation based on the child's developmental age. This approach most often is successful when partners are separating with minimal conflict and are able to arrive at a workable plan for their child.

A mental-health consultant can be used during the divorce process in another way. The attorneys may find that the parents are too conflicted to work effectively toward the divorce and enlist the aid of a mental-health professional to work on anger reduction techniques so the divorce can proceed.

## Mediation

Mediation has become more commonly used to help divorcing partners arrive at a financial agreement as well as a parenting plan. If parents are unable to arrive at a parenting responsibility decision on their own or with a consultant, the next best alternative is mediation, since it keeps the parents involved in the process. Parents should be given the opportunity and the respect to arrive at their own agreement and not become involved in adversarial action too readily.

Attorneys as well as mental-health workers can mediate both property and parenting time. However, it is generally safer to stay with the strength of your helper: use an attorney to mediate property and a mental-health professional to mediate parenting time.

## Family Evaluation and Coordination

A family evaluation is an effort to sort through the information about the family very carefully, see all family members, observe parent–child interactions, administer needed tests, talk with other professional people who know the family, and prepare a recommendation based on all the information. One research article noted that children prefer this approach because they are more often given an opportunity to be involved.

The obvious drawback to a parenting evaluation is that the decision is taken out of the hands of the parents. Sometimes a parenting evaluation is the only way to proceed to a decision in a timely manner. A parenting evaluation is needed when parents are in chronic or intense conflict, as well as when there are major personality or behavioral issues that would interfere with effective parenting and co-parenting.

## Avoiding Psychobabble

Much of what passes for marriage counseling in offices and on television is poorly conceived and poorly practiced. When working with an emotionally disturbed person, therapists sometimes attempt to reduce the patient's guilt, anxiety, and confusion by unconditional acceptance, telling the person simply, "Do the best you can." The purpose is to reduce negative feelings and, in doing so, decrease anxiety, encouraging the person to use his or her best coping skills. Unfortunately, many counselors have not differentiated between the truly emotionally disordered and the vast majority who come to therapy to learn to do better in life. These counselors support the client's point of view, saying, "Whatever you think or feel is right for you," "Just do the best you can," or "Go with your feelings." These represent failed attempts to instill self-esteem. It is at best supportive counseling and will not help you change and mature. The goal of treatment for most people is to learn more productive skills so that life will be more rewarding. It is the therapist's job to challenge, provide insight, encourage, learn, and teach.

## Interviewing Mental-Health Professionals

It is usually helpful to conduct a brief telephone interview with the mental-health professionals you are considering. First, determine whether the person is a marriage therapist, social worker, psychiatrist, or psychologist. At a later time you can call the state licensing board and determine whether the person is licensed and has had any complaints filed and whether any complaints have been founded.

When talking with the mental-health professional, find out that person's area of specialty. Look for someone who has a clear understanding of divorce issues and has experience working with divorced families. Determine the person's hourly rate and estimate of hours to complete the task you are requesting. Ask if the person has any special interest, such as a bias for fathers or for mothers. Ask what procedure the person will use for consultation, mediation, or evaluation. Following are some specific questions to ask:

- What is the telephone number of the state board for your license?
- How long do you find it takes to complete the requested task?

- What does it cost (hours and hourly fee) to complete the task?
- How many times have you worked with a divorced family?
- What do you feel are the best interventions?
- When during the divorce process should these interventions take place?
- Will you see our child, and if so, what sort of questions will you ask?

# CHAPTER 4

---

# Parenting Plans Demystified

D issolving a marriage is a very complicated process. Many confusing feelings emerge. Issues of finances must be resolved. Future plans must be made. Friends and relatives provide input, which is often "friendly fire." Advice is well-meaning but can become merely another burden you must carry.

Because the issues are so complex and confusing, it is very easy for parents to focus on "ownership" of a child: who will get the kids, and when? It is clear that the children will see less of each parent, and the parents will see less of their children. The loss of time is difficult to accept for every family member. Rather than focus on the needs of the child, parents often fight for custody, as if the children were objects to be divided. Parents engage in the child ownership fight with the false belief that there will be a magical solution: a way to divide the child so that the most "deserving" parent will have the most time. Parents sometimes believe that the court will have the wisdom and insight to make a decision all can accept. In truth, all parenting plans are compromises.

Sometimes parents will demand nonschool time or nonsleep time to enhance their quality time. All time with a child is quality time.

When the courts, with the aid of mental-health professionals, assist you in developing a parenting plan, a major consideration will be your past: who has done what for the child throughout the child's life? One of the most important issues is determining your child's major attachment. Attachment refers to a deep, emotional relationship formed when two people have spent time together, are to some degree dependent on each other, and if separated, would grieve. Attachment is not a magical process. It is the sum total of time and care between caretaker and child. It is important for children to remain in close contact with the person to whom they are most attached. The child's security depends upon maintaining this contact. All the parenting tasks add to the sense of attachment, parent-to-child and child-to-parent. The following list of parenting responsibilities clearly demonstrates that there is no such thing as nonquality time.

- Prepare and serve breakfast
- Change diapers
- Clean after vomiting
- Take temperature
- Sit with ill child
- Take on vacations
- Help with chores
- Help with friendships
- Prepare and serve lunch
- Help with sports
- Help with bedtime ritual
- Take to the zoo
- Provide comfort and Band-Aids as needed
- Take to dentist
- Take to counselor
- Supervise school activities
- Provide clear limits
- Provide consequences
- Prepare and serve meals

- Do dishes
- Supervise Internet access
- Supervise homework
- Facilitate TV experience
- Help overcome fears
- Teach to be cautious when needed
- Answer when child asks for advice
- Avoid giving advice unless asked
- Teach new skills
- Act as supervising parent
- Look at wound to see how bad it is
- Listen to five hundred knock-knock jokes
- Console when emotionally injured

And above all, parents must act in a decent and respectable way so that the child learns decency and respect.

The parent who has attended to most of these daily chores is most often the parent to whom the child is most attached.

## Developing a Parenting Plan

The task of developing a parenting responsibility plan at first seems overwhelming. However, there are only a few basic parenting plans to consider. Look at each one, decide the positives and negatives of each as far as the needs of your child are concerned, and discuss your opinions with the other parent. Modify the basic plan that best fits the schedules of your child and each parent.

## Sole Legal and Physical Parenting Plan

In this arrangement one parent has full legal and physical custody, and the other parent has no contact. The usefulness of such a plan is limited to circumstances in which one parent is unable to provide a safe environment for a child, for example because of criminality, drug use, major unresolved emotional disorder, living in another country, and/or running away from responsibility or because of death.

One parent has total control of the child's needs and, if appropriate, can permit safe contact between the child and the other parent. It is more important for children to have a real parent, no matter how impaired, than a make-believe parent. Having no knowledge of a parent, a child will create one. The make-believe parent will usually be all bad or all good. It is usually best for a child to have a real parent, impairments and all, and learn to accept that parent as a real person, albeit in a safe environment, guided, supported, and structured by a responsible parent.

## Shared Legal Parenting and Sole Physical Parenting Responsibilities

Under this plan, parents share the decision-making responsibilities regarding the child in all areas: education, medical care, alternative care, religious training, and so on. However, one parent is not available to share the physical parenting time because of health problems, incarceration (with evidence of going straight), or employment out of the area. The decision-making process must be clearly stated: Will decisions be reached by consensus? Will the parents rely on an arbitrator? Will one parent make all the decisions and the other only provide advice?

## Shared Legal and Physical Parenting Responsibility: The Options

- *One home-based parent—child with the other parent frequently but briefly*
  This plan is used when the child is very young—in the infant and toddler stages. The child is with the most attached parent to provide a safe, secure home. The child needs ongoing interaction with the other parent. The child will have increased time with this parent as the child matures and can move from home to home without damage. This plan will permit the child to develop an attachment with both parents.

- *One home-based parent—child with other parent every other weekend, from Friday after school to Monday before school, and one weekday evening*

This plan is most effective when one parent works long hours. It is effective when the child needs a "home base."

- *One home-based parent—child with other parent every other weekend, from Thursday or Friday after school to Monday or Tuesday before school*
  This plan permits the second parent an opportunity to participate in school activities, assist with homework, and facilitate extracurricular activities.

- *Parents assume equal responsibility for parenting time, exchanging the child every three and a half days*
  Such a plan requires the child to frequently move and is not advisable unless it meets the specific schedule of a family; parents live near each other, in the same school district; and there is minimal conflict.

- *Parents have equal responsibility for parenting time, developing a "two-five" schedule*
  The child will always be with one parent on Mondays and Tuesdays, with the other parent on Wednesdays and Thursdays, and with one parent on alternating long weekends. It is not as complicated as it sounds, and parents who live near each other and are not in intense conflict report that it permits the child to develop effective routines. The negative aspect is that the child lives out of a suitcase.

- *Parents have equal responsibility for parenting time, exchange occurring once a week*
  Parents report that this plan can be made to work if the parents live near each other, are not in intense conflict, and can communicate well about their child. The major complaint comes from a child who wants/needs a home base.

- *Parents assume equal responsibility for parenting time, with exchange occurring monthly, bimonthly, quarterly, every half year, or yearly*
  The drawbacks are obvious. A child settles into an environment and then must make a major readjustment when moving to the home of the other parent. It is a plan that is rarely used except when parents have special needs.

## Percentages Mean Nothing to Your Child

As you sort through these alternatives, you will find that some simply do not meet your needs, but others are possibly workable. Although child support is often based on the percentage of time a child has with each parent, such a factor has no bearing on the well-being of your child. Regardless of the parenting plan, child support should be paid by fund transfer, from either a payroll account or a bank.

Some plans are helpful when one parent has major behavioral, emotional, or character problems. Some work best for infants or toddlers. Some are most effective for school-age and adolescent children.

List the pros and cons for each plan, and then review your answers with the other parent to determine if they are to meet your needs or your child's needs.

# CHAPTER 5

---

# Your Child during the Transition

Your child will react to the transition of living in two homes based on four factors:

1. How you as parents present the information
2. Your child's personality
3. Your child's developmental age
4. Consistency

## Assisting Your Infant Child's Transition to Two Homes

Your infant child cannot talk or even understand what you say. But your child will feel and react to what is happening. If an infant is removed from a parent's care for a prolonged period of time, the image of that parent will begin to fade, and the child might well experience a sense of loss. Your infant may react to a change in schedules, food, voices, and moods. To ensure that your infant child has an easy transition, consistency is the watchword. Permit your child to remain with the most attached parent. The other parent should have brief but frequent parenting times.

Arranging for the other parent to visit is often difficult for parents who are in the process of divorcing. Yet it is in the best interest of your infant child for you to do so. Arrange clearly defined times, such as Monday, Thursday, and Saturday from 3:00 p.m. to 4:00 p.m., for the other parent to be with the child. The attached parent can remain nearby and go to another room or, when it is clear the parenting time is not stressful to the child, use the time to go to the store or visit friends.

An infant can feel anger and anxiety and react to it. If one parent or the other is unable to manage feelings, then the other parent should have sole physical and legal responsibility.

## Assisting Your Preschool Child's Transition to Two Homes

Children at this age are unreasonable; that is, they can't reason. They will put together ideas that really aren't related. One little boy I knew turned on the light in his room just when there was a big thunderclap outside. He was convinced turning on the light had caused the thunderclap. Once he had that idea in mind, it was difficult for him to accept that one event had nothing to do with the other. Although toddlers may not understand the complex reasons for divorce, they will be very aware of what is happening.

I asked a preschooler how she found out her parents had decided to live in two houses. She said, "I heard them divorcing. They divorced all night long."

A child needs to be prepared for changes brought about by divorce. Parents will often prepare a child for kindergarten by walking the child to school, walking through the classrooms, talking with the teacher, attending a get-acquainted party, and reading books about the first day of school. Parents who are "divorcing all night" may forget to prepare the child for parental separation, for living in two houses instead of one, and for spending time away from each parent. Telling your child about the separation is not easy. Both parents are upset and grieving. Both are hurt and angry. Both are scared and defensive. With all these bad feelings going on, it is understandable that parents may say the wrong things. If you can, tell your child together. You can say something like, "We decided that we will all be happier if Mom and Dad live in different houses. Dad (or Mom) is going to live in a nice apartment (or house). We want you to see his (or her) new place as soon as possible."

The next step is introducing the child to the new home. Let's say that Dad is moving to an apartment. The parents arrange for the father to be at home in his new apartment, and Mom tells the child, "We are going to see Dad's new place." Mom responds to any questions the child has—"Will I see you again?" "What happens if you get mad at me?" "Does Dad have a girlfriend?" "Are you sad?" "Are you mad?" "Are you glad?" "Don't you want to be with me?" "What if Dad won't let us in?"

Upon arriving at the new residence, Mom or the child rings the doorbell. New boundaries are already being formed, so each parent must be given permission to enter the other parent's home. The child will usually be overwhelmed, either becoming very passive and quiet or acting up. It is easy at this point to direct attention to the child, but doing so will intrude on the child's need to observe. Mom and Dad need to talk with each other courteously. A script can be prepared in advance, or the parents can just remember to talk about neutral topics. As the child begins to move around and ask questions, notice what he or she is interested in and talk about it. Answer questions briefly and honestly.

When your child's desire to explore becomes apparent, one or both of you take your child outside, see if other children are around, and see if there is a playground or a pool. After a half hour or so, Mom and the child say good-bye and leave.

A few days later, Mom and the child return to Dad's new home for lunch. When the child is comfortable, Mom might say, "I have to go to the store. I will be back real soon." Mom leaves, and Dad and child talk, play, and explore. Do not go into elaborate detail. Be matter-of-fact. If your child becomes frightened and does not want the visiting parent to leave, cut the visit short and plan another visit together. Remember that children learn by association (turning on a light will cause thunder). If you rush the process, your child may make a very negative association with the new home. It is better to make three or four visits together than have your child afraid of being with one parent or the other.

When Mom has left and the child asks questions, give brief answers. Mom must return before she said she would. This is not the time to get held up in traffic or be late for any reason. Your child is still dealing with separation problems and needs not only reassurance but also proof of ongoing security. Mom and Dad can talk for a minute, and then Mom will say, "Let's go to your other home," and the Mom and child then leave. It is normal for a toddler to grieve—to cry, to miss the other parent, to be quiet at times, to look sad, and to feel overwhelmed. Each parent is grieving in his or her own way, and it is okay for the child to do so as well. If you notice any problems or believe your child is feeling uncomfortable, repeat the brief daytime parenting. Do not move on to the next step until this becomes a pleasant part of your child's life. Some parents are concerned that if a child cries and a visit is cut short, the child is manipulating or trying to control the situation. This is rarely the case. A crying child is usually upset. It is better to be cautious than for your child to develop anger toward one or both parents.

If your child becomes extremely agitated, stop what you are trying to do and remove the child from the source of concern. Later, listen carefully to your child to see what is causing the concern. It is very easy at this point to blame the other parent. However, the cause of the problem is usually the changes in the family. Trying to force the exchange could cause the child to become even more frightened and reject one of the parents. Restart the program, go slowly, and help your child make this important adjustment.

The next step is to plan for your child to be with the other parent overnight once both parents are sure the child is comfortable with the daytime meetings. Tell your child he or she will be spending the night with Dad in the new house. Young children cannot tell time, so phrase comments in language the child can understand: "Dad is coming just before dinner tonight. He has invited you to have dinner with him and to sleep over with him in his new house. You get to have breakfast with him too. Then I will come and pick you up." This is not a time for either parent to have a significant other with them. It is extremely important to make these transitions go smoothly, to make the experience pleasant for your child.

## Assisting Your Grade-School Child's Transition to Two Homes

Telling a seven-year-old about divorce is fraught with peril. A seven-year-old will appear to understand what you are saying but often really doesn't understand. Your child will possess the needed vocabulary, will have seen TV shows about divorce, and will have talked to friends about divorce. However, a grade-school child really cannot comprehend the complexities of falling in love, falling out of love, what is for their "own good" and why living in two homes will "make things better." To make matters more complicated, your grade-school child will have keenly observed parental interactions and overheard adult discussions.

For example, a seven-year-old may be told that Mom and Dad aren't going to live together because they don't love each other anymore. This is a common explanation given to a small child, but one that can be misunderstood. A child may ask, "What will happen if you don't love me anymore?" You carefully explain that a parent's love for a child is different from parents' love for each other. But a small child just can't understand that concept. It is usually better not to give a grade-school child too much information to distort. For example, say, "Mom and Dad decided we would all be happier if we lived in two houses."

It is possible to be straightforward, explaining that a parental decision has been made to have two households. But it is crucial to give your child an opportunity to ask questions and make comments. If you don't, your grade-school child may assume questions and comments are not permitted. Find out what your child is thinking. Listen for distortions. For example, one nine-year-old boy overheard his father say his mother would "be the death" of him. The boy, taking his father's words literally, thought he was going to die.

Upon being told about the separation, a grade-school child may respond in several ways. Consider the following examples:

Parents: "Mom and Dad have decided that we will be happier if we live in two different houses, and you get to go from one home to the other."

Child: "Okay."
Parent: (no response)

Child: "Why?"
Parents: "There are a lot of grown-up reasons, but for right now, it is important for you to know that you will be with each of us, and we both love you."

Child: "It won't make me happy!"
Parents: "You are right. It won't make you happy right now, but you will be okay."

Child: "Do you get two houses when you fight all the time?"
Parents: "Fighting did have something to do with our decision. We want all of us to be happy, and we can't do that if we are fighting all the time."

Grade-school children are often embarrassed about the divorce and need help in telling their friends. Do not fight in front of your child or in front of your child's friends. Just don't.

Take responsibility for the tasks associated with moving the child back and forth. Any ten-year-old can tell you how complicated it is to get up in the morning, get dressed, and go to school. To ask a child to do these exhausting tasks and then tell him or her to pack a suitcase often presents an insurmountable obstacle. Do not put your divorce burdens on your child. You pack the suitcase. You clarify schedules. You call the other parent. You prompt needed telephone calls.

A grade-school-age child has difficulty with exchanges. It is the moment when parents again come together. Children feel discomfort; they want their parents to reunite but are reminded once again they will not. Do not place your burdens on your child. You go to the other parent's door. You speak to the other parent civilly. You carry the suitcase. You make sure your child is comfortable. Most important, tell your child it is okay to ask questions and to make comments. You may not like what you hear, but that is your burden, not the child's.

## Telling a Teenager about Separation

Your teenage child will already know most of the details about the separation but will need to be told anyway. A teenager has the capacity to listen and understand. However, a teenager does not have a lot of past experience to fall back on. Explain that you have decided to separate, assure your child it is a no-fault situation, and then listen very carefully. Give your child permission to talk, ask questions, make statements, feel emotions, grieve, become angry, and be goofy. Teenagers will sometimes decide they must take sides and need to be reassured this is not required.

Teenagers will sometimes avoid conflict by self-emancipation, hanging out entirely with friends and avoiding both homes. Let your teenager know that you expect continued involvement in each home. It may be apparent to you, but a teenager needs to be told how to act: your teenager doesn't have to be mad at either parent or try to take care of either parent. Your teenager may need to be reassured you won't starve to death, and so on.

Do not assume that the adjustment to two homes is going to be easy. A teenager, if nothing else, is a traditionalist. The move will disrupt old routines and can be quite traumatic. Teenagers are like cats in two important ways: If you call them, they won't come. And if you change their environment, they get testy. Help your teen with the move. Give your child extra time to talk and to ask questions.

You may be inclined to make your teen a confidant, sharing all the problems of the marriage and divorce. Don't do this. It is too much of a load for anyone.

## An Executive Meeting for All Ages

Within a few days, you, as parents, need to talk to each other about your child's reaction. The discussion should be held when the child is not present. Using a checklist helps:

- What questions or comments did the child make about the new arrangement?
- Did the child appear agitated, upset, worried, or angry?
- Did the child have an appetite for the next few meals?

43

- Did the child go to bed okay that evening? Bad dreams? Bed-wetting?
- Did the child have temper tantrums or show other signs of being upset?

# CHAPTER 6

---

# A Model Parenting Plan

Arla's parents separated when she was four years old. They worked with a mediator, who helped them focus on Arla as a four-year-old and construct a parenting plan to meet her needs through the grade-school years. There are several goals when putting together an effective parenting plan.

- The plan should reduce conflict between parents.
- The plan should take into consideration the capacity of each parent to provide a safe environment and to permit the child to have easy access to both parents.
- The plan should provide consistency and structure for the child throughout a developmental stage.

The following plan for Arla strives to meet these goals. Yet there has never, to my knowledge, been a parenting plan so clear that no misunderstandings occurred.

## Definition of Terms

Home-based parent:     The parent who has the majority of the parenting time

Responsible parent:     The parent who is immediately responsible for Arla

Other parent:     The parent who does not have immediate responsibility for Arla

## Establishing Parental Responsibility

The parents shall provide safe homes for Arla as follows:

Mother shall be the home-based parent through the grade-school years, to be reviewed just before Arla enters junior high.

Father, who has established a home in the same school district, will have parenting responsibility for Arla every other weekend from Thursday after school to Monday before school.

When school is not in session, exchange times will correspond to the school schedule.

## Vacation Planning

The key to effective vacations is cooperation between parents. The exact times, addresses, and telephone numbers shall be agreed upon in writing. Vacations will occur during school breaks, accommodating each parent's special time with the child. Parents agree that on special occasions, if Arla's behavior warrants it, a parent may, with a minimum of two weeks' notice, plan a trip that will involve Arla missing school. Such a plan must be made in cooperation with her teacher.

In the absence of a written agreement one month before the vacation, Mother will have a one-week uninterrupted vacation period with Arla the second week of July, starting Friday after school and ending a week later on Monday before school. Father will have a one-week uninterrupted vacation period with Arla the second week of August, starting Friday after school and ending a week later on Monday before school.

When Arla is seven years of age, or sooner if parents agree in writing, the vacation period will be extended to two weeks.

Parents will prepare Arla for the extended time away from each parent, utilizing their parenting skills and if necessary the assistance of a child therapist. If a phone is available, Arla will be assisted in making a telephone call to the other parent each Wednesday evening or another evening if agreed upon in writing by the parents in advance.

If Arla becomes overwhelmed by the change in her schedule and is frightened, sad, confused, or otherwise upset, parents will hold an information call and determine a course of action. It should be noted that advanced preparation usually will result in nonproblematic vacationing for a child four or older.

## Socialization

Arla shall not be spanked unless both parents agree in writing that this is their preferred form of discipline. No other person, including stepparents, significant others, or grandparents, shall be involved in the physical discipline of Arla. Parents shall share their philosophies of discipline.

## Clothing

Parents shall maintain one wardrobe for Arla. She will have the option, with the assistance of a parent, to move her clothing from one home to the other. As clothing becomes unevenly distributed, the parents will meet and exchange Arla's clothing, avoiding placing her in the position of handling the clothing issues that were brought about by the parents' desire to separate. Arla's clothing shall be purchased from the support money provided by father and allocated by mother. The parents have agreed that a normal clothing allowance for Arla is $100.00 a month, $1,200.00 a year. Either parent may purchase clothing that will then be part of Arla's common wardrobe. Mother will collect clothing receipts and give them to father every quarter (March, June, September, and December).

If an expensive item is lost, stolen, or damaged, parents will share equally in the replacement cost. Parents shall not blame each other or Arla for the normal attrition of clothing or for lost clothing. Each parent shall have the responsibility to maintain Arla's wardrobe, including washing, drying, ironing, dry-cleaning, and mending. Clothes in disrepair will not be transferred from one home to the other. Arla's school uniforms will be maintained by each parent.

## Parental Availability

Each parent shall keep the other parent informed of all co-parenting information, including who is living in each home, address, telephone, place of work, emergency telephone contacts, and care providers.

| Mother | 1234 Happy Street | 555-5555 |
|---|---|---|
| Work | 100 Drudge Street | 444-4444 |
| Emergency | Grandmother Smith | 333-3333 |
| Father | 6389 Okay Avenue | 555-2345 |
| Work | Grind Plaza #101 | 666-6666 |
| Emergency | Sister (Aunt) Gina | 777-7777 |
| Teacher | Ms. Jones | 888-8888 |
| Day care | Ms. Scott | 999-9999 |

## Holiday Schedule

|  | Every Year | Odd Year | Even Year |
|---|---|---|---|
| Martin Luther King's Birthday | | Mom | Dad |
| Presidents Day | | Dad | Mom |
| Spring Break | | Mom | Dad |
| Easter Sunday | | Dad | Mom |
| Memorial Day | | Mom | Dad |
| Mother's Day | Mom | | |
| Father's Day | Dad | | |
| Independence Day | | Dad | Mom |
| Labor Day | | Mom | Dad |
| Halloween | Mom/Dad | | |
| Veterans Day | | Dad | Mom |
| Thanksgiving | | Mom | Dad |
| Winter Break—first half | | Mom | Dad |
| Christmas Eve | | Mom | Dad |

|  | Every Year | Odd Year | Even Year |
|---|---|---|---|
| Christmas Day |  | Dad | Mom |
| Christmas/Winter Break—second half |  | Dad | Mom |
| Child's birthday | Mom / Dad |  |  |
| Mother's Birthday |  | Mom |  |
| Father's Birthday |  |  | Dad |

## Logistics: Cooperative Co-parent Planning

The following schedule shall be followed. Any changes shall be in writing, dated and signed by both parents indicating agreement to the changes, executed one week before the initiation of the changes.

- All three-day weekends begin when school is out on Friday and end when school commences on Tuesday.
- Spring break begins when school is out on Friday and ends when school commences on Monday at end of spring break.
- Easter begins Friday and ends Monday unless it falls in other parent's spring break. In that case, Easter parenting time begins Saturday evening and ends Monday morning.
- Independence Day begins on July 3 at 6:00 p.m. and ends July 5 at 9:00 a.m.
- Halloween shall be shared. Arla shall be with the parent whom she usually would be with on October 31, who will assist her in selecting a costume and meeting social obligations. Arla will be with the other parent for thirty minutes, either at that parent's house or at the house in which Arla is staying.
- Thanksgiving parenting time begins Wednesday evening after school and ends Monday before school.
- The first half of winter break begins when school is out and ends 7:00 p.m. Christmas Eve.
- The second half of winter breaks begins 7:00 p.m. Christmas Eve and ends when school resumes.

- Parents agree that Arla's birthday will be celebrated at the responsible parent's home. The other parent (and stepparent) is invited to attend.
- Parents' birthdays will be celebrated with Arla from after school until 7:00 p.m. If no school is in session, then the celebration with the nonresidential parent will be from 3:00 p.m. to 7:00 p.m.

Responsibility for providing transportation shall be that of the receiving parent. If Arla becomes upset regarding exchanges, then the parent relinquishing Arla will provide the transportation to give Arla a sense of active involvement in the exchange.

The exchanges will take place at school when school is in session, at the home of the care provider if a parent is not available, or at either parent's home.

If school is not in session, school time will be observed for the exchange. The only topic of conversation between Arla's parents at the time of exchange will be to ease her moving from one home to the other.

For purposes of vacation and holiday time, Arla may be removed from the state of California with two weeks' written notice with written information as to purpose of trip, whereabouts, and contact telephone numbers.

Arla shall be prepared for the exchange, and the exchange shall occur unless the parents agree in advance and/or her pediatrician states that she is unable to travel because of illness or injury.

## Alterations of the Parenting Plan

The other parent has the right of first refusal to care for Arla if the responsible parent is unable to care for Arla for a period extending overnight.

If the responsible parent is unable to care for Arla, the other parent may provide that care. No makeup time will be scheduled.

When parents and Arla attend the same function, change of responsible parenting will occur for a period of five to ten minutes. Arla will see the other parent and want to greet that person. Parents will make eye contact, and the responsible parent will find seating for self and child. The other parent will, within a few minutes, return Arla to the responsible parent, make a positive comment, and return to own seat.

## Medical, Dental, and Psychological Care Provision

Father will provide medical insurance. Necessary cards will be provided to mother. The insurance carrier is Health America (HA), and the card number is 123456789.

Marcus Wallaby, MD, 60 Merry Lane, telephone 666-6666, the primary physician, will provide routine medical care.

Samuel Smiles, DDS, 61 Merry Lane, telephone 111-1111, the primary dentist, shall provide dental care.

Each parent shall attend to any child emergency and, at the soonest possible time, inform the other parent. Each parent can obtain emergency medical/dental care as needed.

Each parent will be informed by the other parent in advance of any routine medical/dental appointment, may attend each medical/dental appointment, and shall provide the care outlined by the provider.

Psychological care shall be agreed upon by the parents. Both parents will work with the mental-health provider to assure appropriate parental involvement and appropriate treatment for Arla. Neither parent may take Arla to another mental-health provider without the knowledge and consent of the other parent and the primary mental-health provider.

## Easy Access to Child

Parents will agree upon a time for a daily call by the other parent to the responsible parent's home to talk with the child for five minutes (or with multiple children, for five minutes with each child). If parents are unable to agree upon a time, or do not wish another time, the following schedule will be followed. The other parent may call Arla at the responsible parent's home every day between the hours of 5:00 p.m. and 7:00 p.m. If the responsible parent knows Arla will not be available at that time, that parent will assist Arla in making the call at another time that same day.

Arla may call the other parent any time except when eating, getting ready for bed, or avoiding appropriate parental confrontation.

Telephone calls shall be arranged to avoid interference with study time, meals, and bedtime.

Parents will discuss Arla's feelings, attitudes and comments about such telephone calls during their weekly telephone call.

## Schooling and Day Care

Arla is currently enrolled in day care three mornings a week with Ms. Scott.

Arla will begin school at the age of five years and one month. The school she will attend is Complimentary Elementary at 81 College Lane, telephone 999-1000. Parents, stepparents, and significant others may attend any school function, including programs and teacher conferences.

Parents will determine who will accompany the child on each field trip.

Parents will arrange with the school to receive copies of all notices and reports. A parent, upon receipt of a school notice and/or report, shall send a copy to the other parent.

Parents have agreed upon the school Arla will attend. If there is a change of circumstances, and in the absence of agreement as to which school she will attend, an objective educational adviser shall be consulted to determine Arla's educational needs. Parents have agreed that Ms. Scott will be the sole day care provider. Neither parent shall form an independent alliance or engage in a power struggle with the provider. In the event parents are unable to agree or problems occur, parents shall consult a mediator or a special master to determine an appropriate day care provider.

## Co-parent Decision Making

Parents will make every effort to reach a mutual decision on child issues during their weekly telephone call.

If an issue arises that takes more than two minutes, a time will be scheduled for a thirty-minute telephone call to discuss the issue.

Prior to the thirty-minute decision-making session, parents will collect the needed information to make an informed decision.

If parents are unable to make a decision during the thirty-minute decision-making session, they will contact a mediator for a session to make the needed decision. Parents will supply needed information to the mediator in advance.

The mediation session will last no longer than two hours. If parents are unable to agree after working with a mediator for two hours, they agree to return to court for a full hearing on the issue or hire a special master to make the decision for them and teach them additional decision-making skills.

Either parent can invoke mediation, paying the cost of the first hour, with each parent paying one-half the cost of subsequent hours.

## Remedial Programs

Neither parent has a problem with addiction. No remedial program is indicated. Neither parent has an anger control problem. No such program is indicated.

Arla is a reasonable, well-adjusted child and does not need counseling at this time.

Arla's parents have managed exchanges appropriately, and supervised exchanges are not needed. Father believes that a child may need an occasional spanking. Mother is against spanking. Parents agree that neither parent will spank Arla. Both parents will independently take a parenting course at Mercy Hospital to increase their parenting skills.

Parents agree to commence the Shared Parenting Support Program, attending ten sessions, working with S. Young, Ph.D., who is held to confidentiality.

Parents have demonstrated a propensity to avoid decisions and to argue rather than make the necessary decisions for Arla. If their ability does not improve through the Shared Parenting Support Program, then they have agreed to accept a special master, who will have quasi-judicial authority regarding the subjects of which school to attend, homework practices at each home, orthodontic care, and counseling.

## Long-Term Planning

The present plan, agreed upon by both parents or determined by the court, shall commence on January 1. The present plan should be reevaluated, based on Arla's developmental age, in the summer before she enters junior high school, or when there has been a significant change of circumstances prior to that time.

Should one parent plan to move closer than two miles to or farther than twenty miles from the other parent, notice shall be given, and the parents shall discuss the plan.

Should one parent plan to move out of the county, the other parent shall be given sixty days' written notice in advance and agree to revise the court-ordered parenting plan as needed based on the needs of the child. If the moving parent must leave before sixty days, the child will be with the parent remaining until a long-term plan is developed.

The parent considering moving shall have the financial responsibility for move-away mediation and carry the burden of proof that the move is in Arla's best interest.

# PART 2

## Managing Complex Emotions

Part 2 includes cautionary tales and discussions of how to manage emotions, including how to avoid meltdowns, recover from them, and understand why they occur.

# CHAPTER 7

---

# Managing Anger

If a year after your divorce is final you find that you are still angry, your anger is unproductive and only hurting you and your child. This chapter covers some things you can do to manage your anger so that your child won't be hurt.

## Replace Bad Feelings with Good Feelings

When parents are in the process of divorcing, they often become overwhelmed with problems, hurts, and conflicts. It is easy to get into a rut, thinking only of these important but negative issues. Your thinking becomes catastrophic. You can see no way out of the problems, and you imagine the worst possible scenarios.

You can practice replacing the catastrophic feelings with positive feelings, developing a mantra, a chant, or a visualization in which you imagine a positive outcome. Think of what you want to accomplish. Think of good times that will occur when you set aside the conflict. Think of your skills and abilities. Think of how much better off your child will be when you control your co-parent anger. By doing so, you will relieve yourself of some of the pressure you have been feeling. You can then go back to the tasks of co-parenting—successfully solving problems.

## Keep Your Goals Clearly in Mind

Parents often become angry when they are confused about the new type of relationship they must have with the other parent. All the old intimate feelings don't just fade and go away. Parents, experiencing the return of old intimate feelings, become frightened and then use anger to regain distance. You can remind yourself that it is all right to keep your old feelings of intimacy. You will occasionally notice those old feelings reemerging. It is healthy to remember the good times, proving you are capable of a healthy, happy relationship. Your goal is to move past anger to the business of co-parenting.

## Assure Safety

When parents separate, one or both may feel unsafe because of the amount of anger that is expressed and the threats, real or implied, that have been made. It is important to maintain very clear boundaries and limits. No parent should accept being physically, verbally, or emotionally abused by the other parent. If you feel unsafe, remove yourself from the situation. If violence is threatened, make sure of your own safety and the safety of your child and then call the police.

Learn from your experience what you can and cannot say to the other parent. When you can safely reflect on what happened, realistically assess the degree to which you contributed to the unsafe situation and to what degree the situation was truly unsafe.

## No Longer Rely on the Other Parent for Approval

One of the more difficult emotional changes is to no longer need the approval of the other parent. After separation, it is not easy to give up this need. You will want to rehash the past and get the other parent to agree with your view of the problems. Most arguments are about old issues that will never be solved. When you argue about who was responsible for the separation and whose problems were the causes of the divorce, anger will only increase. The more you can talk about the present and the future, the less you will have to argue about.

## Be Specific

Keep your discussions focused on clearly defined goals, such as how to provide for two houses, how to communicate about your child, and what to do about schooling, medical/dental care, counseling, and all the issues relevant to co-parenting. Nothing will start an argument faster than vague accusations—for example, "You always leave everything to the last minute" or "You never bring our child back on time." Following is a more specific comment that could reduce anger: "Last Monday when you returned Dexter, it was 8:30 rather than 8:00. As a result he was late for school. Would you please make sure he is here by 8:00 so he can get to school on time?"

## Specify a Satisfactory Outcome

Make sure you know what the other parent is trying to communicate. Listen carefully and, if needed, ask for clarification. What specifically does that parent want, and how will you know if it is available? For example, Mom might say, "Our child will need enough money to live on." She may be thinking of half of the family income. Dad may think she is talking about 90 percent of the family income. It is much more productive for each parent to prepare a budget and give specific amounts. There is little chance that warring parents will agree on what is "enough money to live on." State clearly what you want. Listen clearly to what the other parent wants and negotiate an agreement.

## Teach Yourself to Be Calm

When you feel yourself becoming angry, take a moment to calm yourself. You have that ability. Take a deep breath, hold it for a few seconds, and then slowly release it. Repeat several times. While doing so, tell yourself that you are calm and clearheaded, and your goal is to communicate clearly, discuss the needs of your child, and move on with your life. If you feel tingly or agitated, that is often because you have breathed too rapidly. The key is to breathe slowly and deeply.

## Determine Your Vulnerability

Parents often become angry when a personal weakness is revealed. If you feel you are poor at sports and always wanted to be a great football player, you may react with anger if someone points out that you are a klutz. If you knew and accepted that you lacked musical skills, and someone said that you would never be a concert violinist, you might simply agree because not becoming a concert violinist is not something that makes you feel vulnerable.

Each of us has feelings of weakness and vulnerability, which, when mentioned by others, makes us fighting mad.

A new teacher ran into the principal's office and, very agitated, said, "Johnny just called me an SOB. What should I do?" The old principal leaned back in his chair and said, "First, decide if you are."

Once you decide whether what you are accused of is true or false, you can take action. If it is true and you have made a mistake, admit it, thank the other person for free therapy, and move on. You may, if you wish, try to change that aspect of yourself. If it is not true, try to understand how the untrue idea came about. In either case, it is an opportunity to see what makes you angry and find new ways to resolve your anger.

## Give Yourself a Safety Valve

Be aware of when you are becoming angry. Understand that you cannot work your best when angry. Learn to give yourself a safety valve. In the Shared Parenting Support Program, the safety valve is the phrase "I am overwhelmed." You are acknowledging the problem is yours. You can then take the time you need to regain control: take a break, terminate the discussion, or move on to another topic—whatever helps you to manage your angry feelings. Saying, "You make me angry" is always counterproductive. It is placing responsibility for your feelings on the other parent, thereby giving up control and responsibility.

## Be in Control of Yourself

Sometimes anger is a luxury you can't afford. Don't indulge in useless anger. We live in a society that is based on rules. There are laws to back up many of these rules, but rarely do we need policemen around to make sure we are being law-abiding. Being civilized assumes we each can control our behavior. If a person can't control his or her behavior, that person is excused because of physical or psychological issues. Other than these exceptions, we are responsible for our own behavior. Sometimes parents who are dissolving their relationship become very angry and want to be an exception to the rule of personal responsibility. You must control your own anger, focus on the needs of your child, and act with civility. The key question when interacting with the other parent is, "How will the words I use, the ideas I express, the emotions I show, and the behaviors I act out help my child?" Parental conflict is not helpful to a child. It is harmful. Threatening, bullying, and cajoling the other parent hurts your child. If you find you are unable to control the expression of your feelings, seek appropriate treatment for the well-being of yourself and your child.

## Talk in Paragraphs

Parents must not both talk at the same time. I have heard otherwise competent parents and stepparents all talk at the same time. Doing so is counterproductive. If everyone talks at once, no one will hear anyone else. If you are talking at the same time the other parent is talking, you have quit listening, formulated your response, and begun talking before you have heard and acknowledged the other parent's point of view, thus totally blocking any real communication.

In the Shared Parenting Support Program, one basic rule is that co-parents will talk in paragraphs. Each parent should be able to express an entire thought without interruptions. If a paragraph goes on for more than a few minutes, communication has again broken down and becomes a monologue. Acknowledge to yourself that you are overwhelmed and then say out loud, "I would like to respond now." Finding a neutral, respectful, assertive way of establishing your rights is something you can practice before talking to the other parent.

## Inform—Don't Try to Persuade

A basic rule of shared parenting is that 99 percent of the time co-parents simply need to exchange information—not to persuade the other parent to change a point of view. The difference is very basic.

*An Example of Exchanging Information*

You:      Johnny made an A in math today. He is doing really well.
Other:    Great!
You:      [To yourself] Well, that went well!

*An Example of Trying to Persuade*

You:      Johnny made an A in math today!
Ex:       Great!
You:      I have probably told you a hundred times that he needs a private school.
Ex:       It sounds like you believe he needs to be in a private school. The teachers say he is doing well where he is. Also, I can't afford a private school. If you want to talk about making a change, let's work with a mediator to see what we can do.
You:      [Embarrassed that the other parent handled it better than you did] Why, you!

## Talk without Major Distractions

Set aside time to talk with each other about co-parenting issues so that your views will be clearly expressed. Co-parents can become so conflicted that they rarely talk to each other, and when they do, they have so much to cover, they talk too fast about too many issues.

## Understanding Impasse Issues

When two people first get together, they agree on almost everything. As their marriage matures, they find that they do have differences, which is normal. These differences can be overlooked in favor of the positive aspects of being together. Like all couples, they have "impasse issues." Those are differences that cannot be reconciled.

As the relationship deteriorates, there are fewer and fewer positives in the relationship, and the impasse issues become increasingly important and finally are all that is left. That is usually the point when parents separate. Their relationship consists of fights over impasse issues. Learn to step away from an impasse issue, realizing it is futile to argue about issues that will never be resolved.

## Ten Signs to Help You Know You Are Dealing with an Impasse Issue:

1. You forget what you were arguing about but keep on arguing.
2. You have vague feelings of having had the same argument many times.
3. You become bored with the argument but keep on arguing.
4. You want to persuade rather than inform.
5. You forget that problems are solved by effective communication.
6. You believe that if you talk loudly and fast, you can convince the other parent that you are right.
7. You feel helpless.
8. You feel rage.
9. You forget that anger has nothing to do with effective problem solving.
10. You mention that the other parent is just like his or her mother.

## How to Avoid Impasse Issues

When you find yourself involved in a repetitious conflict with the other parent and have scored five out of the ten signs of an impasse issue, appreciate that you are not going to solve the issue. Gracefully move on. Imagine there is a ten-ton boulder, painted pink, sitting in the middle of the road on your way to work. Every day when driving to work, you run into this boulder. Sooner or later, you are going to decide that it is in your best interest to detour around the boulder, saving time, energy, and peace of mind. Think of the impasse issues as ten-ton boulders. Some people are able to see their impasse issues readily, and others are not. In the Shared Parenting Support Program, one of the main tasks of the therapist is to identify impasse issues and, when they occur, remind the parents to steer around them. When working on your own co-parenting skills, learn to recognize impasse issues.

## Seeking Help

If you discover that you cannot control your anger, it is appropriate to attend an anger-control class. There are many organizations and colleges that offer such classes. Check with your church. Call the welfare department. Call the referral number for mental-health professionals. Within a few minutes, you will have some alternatives to choose from. Not all such classes may be suitable for you. Attend a meeting, and if it is not what you need, go elsewhere until you find a program that fits your needs and your personality. Don't attend a class in which the instructor excuses your anger or one in which the instructor tries to make you feel guilty.

There are two kinds of anger issues: those of the aggressor and those of the victim. If you are the aggressor, be honest with yourself and acknowledge that your style of intimidating others may feel good but is not right. Don't wait until you are forced to attend an anger management class. If you have an anger-control problem, do something about it. If you are the victim of aggression, it is imperative you learn why you permit yourself to be a victim and find ways to place better limits in your relationships. Aggressors and victims have a way of finding each other. You can change if you wish.

## Establishing Priorities

After the separation, when parents are fighting about love, hate, parenting time, money, housing, and other objects of sentimental value, they will sometimes say and do things that are damaging to their child. Their conflict, enhanced by the adversarial process of divorcing, often results in loss of contact with the real issues:

- It is not a question of which parent "deserves" the children.
- It is not a question of which parent will feel the loss more keenly.
- It is not a question of which parent has the "right" to be with their child.
- It is not a time to solve culturally traditional issues.
- It is about the needs of the child to have the best of both parents.

# CHAPTER 8

---

# Polarization: A Defense against Pain

As parents battle over parenting responsibility time, each will use one of the most common defenses against pain: polarization. Parents will polarize their feelings, believing the other parent is totally and completely at fault. Often, each parent, frustrated by the tasks of separating, increasingly believes that he or she is an innocent victim of the malicious other parent.

## Helplessness

The longer the conflict continues, the more polarized each parent can become. When working with a divorced couple, I will ask, "What one thing could you do that would reduce the conflict?" Both parents feel frustrated, unable to think of anything they could do. Often, in despair, one will say, "If I would just go away." The other might say, "If I would just agree with everything that person says."

Then I ask, "What one thing could the other parent do to reduce the conflict?" Each parent can name a hundred things the other parent could do. That is polarization. If you believe the other parent is completely at fault, and things cannot improve until that parent changes, then you must, deep inside, feel helpless.

## Powerlessness

Polarization interferes with parents' ability to effectively talk about the needs of their child. A damaging side effect is that totally blaming the other parent means that you have given away all your power. If you give away all your power, then you can only feel powerless.

## Recovery

To begin your recovery, accept that you are not perfect, that you made mistakes in the past, and that you will undoubtedly make mistakes in the future. Even though it is difficult, fearlessly examine your own behavior and make changes, thus regaining self-control. When you make the changes to improve your co-parenting skills, you will feel more capable of handling problems. When you feel victimized, you can't really feel good about yourself. Although it is hard work to take control of your own life, in doing so you will feel better about yourself.

Sometimes a parent will say that in spite of his or her own changes, the other parent continues to be difficult and cause problems. Take comfort in the knowledge that your child has at least one parent who is making positive decisions.

# CHAPTER 9

---

## Co-parent Paranoia

The conflict often escalates as each parent works to emotionally separate from the person with whom they were intimate and are now intimately angry. It is only natural to avoid conflict and pain. Often it is not comfortable for parents in the transition phase to talk about their children in a rational manner. The one thing they can understand is that by divorcing, each will have less contact with their child—which is bad—and with each other, which is both good and bad. Without understanding the new boundaries, parents do not know how to communicate with each other, how often they should talk, or what they should talk about. Communication, already difficult, often stops.

Without communication, parents can rely only on hunches and guesses about what is happening to their child while in the other home. Because parents are upset and angry, each can make assumptions about the other home that are negative, each believing the worst about the other. Dad wonders if Mom is still occasionally smoking a joint. Mom thinks about Dad's temper, wondering if he is getting very angry with the child.

Wondering but not knowing, guessing, expecting the worst, and avoiding rather than communicating are all part of co-parent paranoia, a condition that needs to be cured as quickly as possible.

The cure is easy to articulate but hard to do: start communicating parent-to-parent, which can be accomplished using the information call, the planning meeting, and the weekly telephone call, all of which are discussed in part 3.

# CHAPTER 10

---

# Child as Communicator

A common problem is for a child to carry messages from one parent to the other. Children have many ways to avoid the burden of carrying messages from parent to parent. Harry, age fourteen, used a typical teenage method.

## Harry's Story

Since his fourteenth birthday, Harry's life had become, you know, bad. Dad had left home, moving to an apartment, saying he had to find himself. "It was, like, sleep with his girlfriend, as if I didn't know," Harry said. "Mom mopes around all day, trying to get me to do the dishes, clean the house, and talk to her when she is lonely and yucky stuff like that. That, like, makes me feel, you know." Mom sat at the kitchen table alone, feeling perplexed. Harry had disobeyed her once again. Since Harry was on his way to visit Dad, all Mom asked was that he remind his father of the court hearing tomorrow.

Meanwhile, Dad and Brigitte started their day at noon with cappuccino, agreeing that they would soon have to get out of bed. Dad was receiving unemployment and Brigitte was receiving child support, so they could enjoy the leisure of true love. They heard the front door open and realized that Harry had arrived. Brigitte told Dad again that he needed to get the locks changed so they could have some privacy. Giving Harry a key had been a big mistake. Putting on a robe, Dad met Harry in the kitchen. Harry was looking through the refrigerator, where he found champagne, chocolates, and a Styrofoam take-out box from a Chinese restaurant.

"Hi, Dad," Harry said, sampling the chocolates. "Wasn't Godiva the one who rode a horse with no clothes on? Our teacher said something about that the other day." Harry laughed. "Actually, it was Godiva that had no clothes on."

"Harry, how many times must I ask you to knock before you come in? Close the refrigerator door. There is nothing in there."

"Okay. Mom said for you to be in court tomorrow morning."

"Oh my God, I forgot all about that. I thought it was next week. Could she get it changed? Tell her I can't make it."

Harry rolled his eyes and went to meet his friends.

Parents realize they must communicate with the other parent, but for many reasons, they decide to communicate through their child. As a result the child becomes the communicator between parents. Both parents were using Harry. His escape from this burden was to spend even more time with his friends. There are several reasons a child should not be used to pass messages from parent to parent.

## Messages under the Best of Circumstances Are Distorted

Even under the best of circumstances, people do not communicate accurately. Most people are familiar with the game of "telephone," in which a line of people whisper a message one to the other until the first and last person announce the message. The messages are always distorted, sometimes with the meaning completely changed.

## Messages Are Distorted When the Messenger Is Anxious

Neither children nor adults can deliver messages accurately when anxious, angry, or distracted. When parents are in conflict, children are not emotionally prepared to deliver messages accurately.

## Overheard Messages Are Always Distorted

When one parent says bad things about the other parent in the presence of the child, the child has been placed in the middle of the parental conflict. Parents often don't realize when they talk inappropriately in front of their child.

It is difficult for parents to understand how often they communicate through their child or how damaging this can be for the child. It is even more damaging when security issues are discussed. References to money make children feel insecure.

## A Child Should Not Be Used to Relay Adult Information

Many parents try to schedule school, extracurricular events, and medical care through the child. The results are uniformly unsuccessful. The child will rarely be able to relay messages accurately. It is even difficult for two adults who are talking directly to communicate well. It is impossible when the message is passed through a child who is worried and concerned about the parental conflict.

## Your Child Manipulates

A child may purposefully distort information. Even in the most functional families, a child will learn to manipulate parents, finding loopholes to rules. A classic example is a child who asks his mother if he can go next door and play with a friend. Mom says, "Go ask Dad." The child goes to Dad in the living room and says, "Mom said it is okay for me to go next door to play with Tommy if it is okay with you." Although subtle and not an important issue, the child was able to manipulate the parents, taking advantage of the lack of direct communication.

## Your Child Even Lies

A major cause of anger between divorcing parents is listening to a child and comparing what the child says with what the other parent is saying or doing. On the basis of this information, one parent calls the other parent a liar. Parents should not assume that a child always reports accurately. Parents have indignantly told me, "My child never lies!" That, of course, is not true, and assuming it is true results in keeping the anger between parents alive and destructive.

## Messages Accurately Transmitted by the Child Can Be Distorted by the Parents

Sometimes the child is able to deliver a message clearly and accurately, and one or both parents will distort the message.

Father says to his eight-year-old daughter, "Ask your mom if she plans to buy you shoes. If not, I'll buy them next week." Daughter reports to her mother, "Dad wants to know if you or he is going to buy me shoes."

Mom angrily replies, "He can't order me around like that. We aren't married anymore!"

## Children May Create Conflict So Parents Will Talk

Sometimes a child will create conflict so parents will talk.

Larry's parents have been divorced for two years, and each has remarried. However, Larry's problems are not yet over. He started acting out in school to relieve some of his stress. He acted out by being late to class and bullying younger children.

He knew he wanted his parents to reunite but had no idea how to make them get back together. He was aware they never talked to each other. They were always saying, "Tell your Mom this," or "Tell your Dad that." Each would grill him at length about the other parent. He also hated the idea of taking a suitcase to school every exchange day. The kids at school were teasing him.

One day, when Larry was packing for his week with his father, he couldn't find any clean clothes. He had more important things to worry about, but he knew his Dad would quiz him about the laundry. He threw all his dirty clothes in the suitcase and lugged it to school and then to Dad's home.

When Larry opened his suitcase, Dad saw all the dirty clothing and bellowed, "What the hell is this about?"

"I don't know," Larry said.

"Don't give me that. Be a man and tell me what your mother has done now," Dad demanded.

"She told me to bring them," Larry whispered.

"She told you to bring dirty clothes? What is she up to now?"

"She said you have a washer and dryer."

"You tell her I am paying enough money for her to buy anything she wants. You are just going to have to wear dirty clothes!" Dad said, stomping off.

When Larry returned to Mom's house, she yelled at him for having dirty clothes. He had developed a plan of sorts and said, "Dad said you can keep my clothes clean."

The next time Mom and Dad got together to exchange Larry, they were yelling and screaming at each other. Larry didn't like the anger but was pleased they were at least talking to each other. Actually it reminded him of the year before his parents separated. He found out that the worse he behaved, the more they talked. They did argue about him, but they were talking and seemed to be getting along as well as ever. Negative attention is often better than no attention at all.

Even though it is at times unpleasant and difficult, parents must develop ways to communicate directly, avoiding making the child the communicator.

# CHAPTER 11

---

# The Child's Paradox

When a child loves two parents who are in conflict with each other, the child is faced with a difficult task: how to love these two, all-important people without taking sides, making them angry, or losing them. That is the child's paradox. The child is concerned that pleasing Dad will make Mom mad, and pleasing Mom will anger Dad. The child is faced with the task of showing love and affection to warring parents.

## A Hypothetical Six-Year-Old Harvard Graduate Sets Her Parents Straight

If the child were attending Harvard rather than grade school and had been through extensive psychotherapy, she might ask to meet with her parents, tell them the parameters of her paradox, and explain what they must do to help her resolve the paradox:

Mom and Dad, I love you both. I don't want to hear you talk about each other in a negative way. You are the only parents I will ever have, and I don't want that taken away from me. I would prefer for you to be together and get along. Lacking that, I am willing to live out of a suitcase and spend as much time as I can with each of you. I am not going to watch every word I say, fearing I will offend you. If I say I love Mom, it is because I do love her, not because I don't love Dad. If I say I love Dad, it is because I do love him, not because I don't love Mom. Now I am going on with my life.

## A Child's Maladaptive Solutions

Unfortunately, children have only maladaptive ways to deal with the paradox of loving two people who are angry with each other. The only solution rests with the parents, who can move past their intimate anger to the business of co-parenting and very carefully permit the child to love each parent individually and unconditionally. There are several ways children attempt to solve the paradox, but none of them will be successful.

## Mara, age twelve, Led Two Lives

One common way children attempt to deal with this situation is to separate life into two parts: time with Dad and time with Mom, never mentioning the absent parent. Many children quickly learn to keep the two homes separate.

Twelve-year-old Mara was very good at reading her mother's facial expressions. It had been difficult for her mother to let go of Mara when she went to spend her first weekend with Dad. When Mara returned from two nights with Dad, she was bathed, her hair was combed, and she had on a clean dress. There was even a bow in Mara's hair, something Dad had never done before. Mara was very excited and happy. "Mommy, Mommy! It was so much fun! We went to the zoo and everything! I hope I can see Daddy real soon!" Mom was crestfallen. She had wanted the visit to go well but also had harbored the fantasy that her daughter would miss her and truly need her. Mom's feelings were reflected on her face. Mara immediately saw that her mother was hurt. Without even thinking about it consciously, she no longer told her mother how much she enjoyed being with her father.

## Faintly Praising One Parent by Slightly Damning the Other

A very common way a child tries to handle the paradox is to say negative things about the other parent. A child has a great need for parental approval.

A child attuned to parents' feelings will soon learn that slightly negative comments about the other parent will make the parent they are with feel better.

Paul had been very embarrassed when Patricia left him for his best friend. No matter how often he told himself that he had to treat Patricia in a businesslike way for the sake of their son, Peter, he was hurt and angry.

Peter, age eight, was aware of the angry and hurt feelings between his parents. He found that he liked his mom's boyfriend, Aaron, which made him feel very guilty. He felt he was betraying his father. He had overheard his dad say it felt like Aaron had stabbed him in the back.

One day, Peter had just returned from Mom's house. He had really enjoyed being with Mom and Aaron. They'd played games, laughed together, and had a good time. But Peter was feeling very guilty, as though he had stabbed his dad in the back.

Dad was watching TV when Peter got home. He said, "Hi, Peter, how was your visit?"

"Okay, I guess," Peter said, not wanting to make Dad feel bad.

"You don't sound very happy. Did anything happen?"

Peter felt trapped now. He said, "Aaron made me do the dishes all alone. That wasn't any fun."

Dad smiled, inwardly relieved that Peter wasn't getting along with Aaron.

Peter noticed the smile and added, "I really don't like stuff like that." He had found a way, although not a good way, to handle the paradox of liking his father and Aaron at the same time.

## Vague Complaints Feeding Co-parent Paranoia

Sometimes a child resents moving from house to house, especially if time with friends is interrupted. When the time comes to leave one parent and go to the other, the child suffers the loss of a parent, friends, and activities but lacks the words to express these feelings accurately.

Six-year-old Robert asked his mom if he could spend Saturday night with his friends who were having a sleepover. Mom said, "But you will be with your dad."

Robert's response was very predictable. "Don't make me go over there."

Mom, assuming the worst said, "Oh? What is going on over there?"

Robert, honestly but vaguely, replied, "Oh, nothing."

## Undivided Loyalty

Sometimes a child will simply take sides, being loyal to one parent and becoming the enemy of the other. Unless one parent is very poor at parenting, this rarely happens. One parent may be encouraging the child to take sides, and the other may not be parenting well. In almost every case, the child's anger at the second parent is based on a real issue. It is almost impossible to alienate a child from a parent unless the parent is missing the parenting boat.

Paula, age eleven, detested living in two homes. She and her mom were very close. They talked together about adult stuff. They went shopping together. They were very happy together. It made Paula feel kind of queasy to hear how bad Dad was, but she could understand. Mom told her that Dad never listened and was always focused on his own needs. "I know!" Paula said. "When I have to go over there, all he does is look at football games on TV." Mom smiled, remembering the lonely Sunday afternoons before she'd come to her senses and left him.

Paula went to Dad's house the next weekend. Dad's new girlfriend, Jennifer, was there. Jennifer and Dad just gazed each other. They would giggle and talk. It was gross. Paula said, "Dad, can we do something?"

Dad said, "I think you have some homework, young lady. Go take care of that." He was proud that he was acting like a real parent, making appropriate demands of his daughter. *Not at all a Disneyland dad*, he thought to himself. Paula felt rejected and ignored. She hated Dad's girlfriend even more.

When Paula returned to her mother's home, she said, "I don't want to go over there ever again."

Mom, swayed by her own angry feelings, said, "You have to be real sure about this. Are you ready to tell the judge how you feel? Are you ready to let the judge know exactly how your dad rejects you all the time? It is up to you. If you are grown up enough to say what you want, we might be able to work it out."

## Placating Parents: The Grown-Up Ploy

Sometimes children will distort how they feel, just to be nice. This is also called the "grown-up ploy." Teachers, scoutmasters, coaches, and others can be caught between warring parents.

The story of Carol, Darlene, and Marilyn is a case in point. Carol, Darlene, and Marilyn were the best of friends. They had attended grade school, high school, and college together. They all lived in the same town and maintained their friendship over the years. Darlene and Marilyn had never agreed on politics or religion. At a party one evening, they had a bit too much to drink, and Darlene joked about Marilyn's political beliefs, making Marilyn very angry. They quit talking to each other, but each talked with Carol.

Carol didn't know what to do. Her two best friends were mad at each other. She didn't want to say anything to hurt their feelings. She didn't want to take sides and lose a friendship. Above all, she was an exceedingly polite person and wanted to do the right thing. Carol had lunch with Marilyn, who said, "I thought Darlene was smarter than that. It was so stupid of her to talk about something she knows nothing about. I can't imagine how I remained friends with her all these years." Carol, wanting to be supportive, said, "Yes, you and she were friends for a long time." Marilyn heard the word "yes" and took it as support.

A few days later, Marilyn was talking with another friend and said, "I talked to Carol about this, and she agrees with me that Darlene is acting stupid." That friend talked with Darlene and said, "You won't believe what Carol said about you."

Although Carol may have tried to remain neutral and not take sides, she was pulled into the argument between friends. Children often find themselves in the same position when faced with warring parents. Children will respond to each parent as they believe each parent wants, leading each parent to believe the children are on their side.

## The Grown-Up Ploy Is Used by Other Adults As Well

John was the new scoutmaster in Roger's troop. He knew that Roger's parents had recently separated and had heard they were fighting in public. Roger's father, Allen, attended a scout meeting and introduced himself to John. John told him that the troop would be going on a camping trip the next weekend. "Uh-oh," Allen said, "that could mean trouble. Roger's mother has parenting time then. You will have to ask her. It is okay with me."

John was uncomfortable, but agreed to ask her, saying, "Yes, I can understand that might be a problem." He thought the parents should coordinate the activity, but he wanted to do a good job as scoutmaster and called Roger's mother, Sally. "Allen said I should call you to coordinate next weekend. He said that Roger can go camping with us."

"He did, did he?" said Sally. "Well, that is my weekend, and I am the one who can give permission for Roger to go camping!"

"Well, I understand that," said John. "Allen may have stepped over the line."

When Sally and Allen talked, Sally said, "John agreed with me that you were out of bounds, giving Roger permission to do something on my weekend."

Allen replied, "He told me that he understood how difficult you might be. That is why he called you."

John was caught in the scoutmaster's paradox as he tried to placate warring parents and lost.

Teachers, scout leaders, pediatricians, dentists, music teachers, day care providers, and other helping adults can be caught in the paradox. However, the adults can go to their own homes and talk about the warring parents. The child, unless he or she has a therapist, may have no one with whom to discuss the problem.

## Carlos Needs a Job

Carlos was a quiet, rather intense eight-year-old who had managed to maintain high grades even though his parents were going through a difficult divorce. We talked for about thirty minutes, and I noticed he was gripping the arms of his chair tightly and was very serious. I said, "Carlos is there anything you would like to ask me?"

He squirmed in his chair and quietly said, "How old do you have to be to work at a hamburger place?"

I told him I wasn't sure but could find out. I thought it was sixteen. "Do you need a job?" I asked him.

"Yeah, Mom isn't going to have any money, and if I don't get a job, she could starve and not have a place to live."

I controlled the urge to say, "Who the hell is feeding ideas like that to you?" and instead said, "That does sound pretty serious. Have you talked to your parents about that?"

"Yeah. Mom. She said Dad was not going to give us enough money to live on." We both squirmed in our chairs for a few minutes.

"Well," I said, "I'm not sure how much child support the judge will decide on, but I can guarantee you won't starve. How about if you and your parents come in, and we will talk about it?"

"Okay."

"You know," I waxed psychologically, "you may not eat caviar for every meal, but I bet both parents will make sure you have a good place to sleep and good food to eat." Our time was about up, and I asked, "Do you have any more questions?"

"Yeah," he said. "What's caviar?"

All children attempt to handle the paradox, and all children fail. The only way out is for the parents to overcome their anger and develop an effective shared-parenting system.

# CHAPTER 12

## The Parental Epiphany

Most families live day by day with little thought to their goals and objectives. If a corporation were to try to manage without goals and objectives, bankruptcy would not be too far behind. Many families who become ineffective and eventually separate have not thought about the future or clearly stated what is best for the family and for each individual in the family. Such planning often only occurs when a major trauma strikes. Persons who narrowly escape death are eager to look at the big picture, understanding that time is finite and living without a plan is wasted time. Parents who divorce often have an epiphany as well: what does the future hold, and how best can the goals and objectives of the newly aligned family be met?

Mom may have worked in a law firm before the child was born, stayed at home for a few months, and then returned to work, putting in an eighteen-hour day: twelve hours at the office and six hours at home. Dad may have started working for the county when he was twenty-five and now at thirty-five may have realized that he is economically stuck. If he were to change jobs, he would lose retirement and have to accept lower pay. As a result, although he is a young man, his life is driven by the needs of a sixty-five-year-old retiree. Although his present course is not bad, it is not what he had wanted. The parents had set aside their dreams: for example, mother to become more involved in the church choir, father to return to his love of fly fishing.

When the trauma of divorce is most intense, parents often realize their lifestyle has taken them away from what they really value, and they think about making changes. Mom may want to stay home with her daughter, who will enter school in a few months. Dad may regret the many hours he has invested in his work at the expense of spending time with his daughter.

A parent may want to make a change, and the other parent may be suspicious of the change. For example, both parents have become accustomed to living on two salaries. Mom may want to cut back on her work as an attorney and spend more time with her daughter. She may well be accused of trying to sabotage Dad. How dare she reduce her income just when there are so many expenses?

Dad may decide he would like to take risks, jump from the county safety net, and spend more time tying flies and writing a book about fly fishing. Mom may be suspicious of his motives, believing he is trying to avoid paying so much child and spousal support. Although a parent may keenly feel the need to leap into a new lifestyle, it is usually most prudent to plan the change over time, making sure the child is living a consistent, predictable, loving life before making changes.

And at the same time, each parent's desire to take stock, look at goals and objectives, and take prudent risks should be honored. A child is probably better off with a prudently risk-taking, part-time attorney, full-time choir-directing mother, if the mother is happy, challenged, and experiencing pleasure in life's daily tasks. A child is probably much better off sitting beside father on a river bank fishing than sitting in day care waiting for a parent tied to a nine-to-five job.

When parents separate, it is often with the belief that doing so will improve the quality of life of the parents and child. Separation can create synergy, making things better than they were before.

# CHAPTER 13

---

## An Example of Making All
## the Wrong Decisions

Jack's parents made all the wrong decisions. Before moving on to how
to solve your problems, use his parents as an example of what not to
do. A list of co-parenting errors follows their harrowing (but not hopeless)
story.

Elliott and Jean had been married almost four years and had a three-year-
old son named Jack. It was each parent's third marriage. They had vowed
they would change all their old bad habits and gain maturity. Each tried to
be on his or her best behavior, but soon the pressure of avoiding fights was
too much. Neither parent was happy, but they didn't know what to do.

Jean returned from a business trip and informed Elliott that she was
leaving. She had just met a man, she said, who was perfect for her, who
would truly take care of her. She wanted to separate so that she and her new
friend, George, could begin living together as soon as possible. She told
Elliott he could have the house, and she would work out an arrangement
so he could see their three-year-old son whenever he wanted. Elliott was
somewhat relieved that the relationship was over, and he hadn't had to

make that decision. He was, of course, hurt, chagrined, embarrassed, and angry too, but still somewhat relieved.

By the next day everyone knew that Elliott and Jean had split, and she was now living with George. People commented that Jean and Elliott had "seemed like such a nice couple," but they were most concerned about their three-year-old son, Jack. "Poor Jack," they agreed.

That weekend, Elliott decided to visit his son. George, whom Elliott had never met, saw him park and met him at his car. "I'm sure you will understand. We just don't want to be disturbed. Jean says she is afraid of you, so please leave."

Elliott left, drove around for thirty minutes, parked, got out his phone and called the police. They asked him for a copy of the court order, which of course he didn't have because one did not exist. Jean had told him he could see Jack whenever he wanted, yet the first time he had tried to see Jack, he was refused—and not by Jean, but by George, who had acted like Jean needed to be protected. Elliot wondered whether Jean could really deny him access to his son.

Elliott saw an attorney Monday afternoon and discovered that Jean really could do that. She could keep Jack away from him. He decided he would think about it a while and not act rashly.

The following week, Jean filed papers stating Elliott had been beating her and "may have been molesting Jack." George's ex-wife had accused him of that, so he knew how effective it was in keeping a father away from his child.

A hearing was set for six weeks later. In the meantime Elliott was granted supervised visitation with his son every Saturday for one hour. Elliott told Jean that his mother would supervise the visits. A few days later, Jean added to her declaration that since the separation, Elliott had not even tried to have visitation with Jack. Furthermore, she declared that during the marriage, he had worked all the time and never spent time with her or Jack. She concluded that Elliott's mother would not be a good caretaker because she was old and forgetful.

Elliott told his attorney that he had tried to see his son, but Jean wouldn't let him. He acknowledged that he did work all the time. He thought it was to provide a living for the family.

The parenting evaluation by a psychologist lasted three months, during which time Elliot had only limited contact with his son. The psychologist and Children's Protective Services could find nothing to support the charges of abuse. However, as any attorney could tell you, you can't unring a bell. The false allegation of abuse can never be disproved—only unsupported. Eventually people seemed to realize that Elliot wasn't just going to go away and was determined to see his son. When the hearing was held, after two more postponements, the court awarded the mother "primary custody" and gave the father "visiting time every other weekend from Saturday morning to Sunday evening."

No one was home when Elliott arrived at Jean's house on Saturday morning as planned. He returned to his home, becoming increasingly angry as he thought about how unfair Jean was being. He called her every hour, leaving increasingly angry messages on her mobile phone. When he called at 3:00 p.m., Jean answered the phone, breathlessly saying they had just returned from Great America, and Jack, who "really loves George," was tired, needed a nap, and didn't want to see Elliott. Elliott angrily demanded his parenting time. Jean said, "I'm sorry it didn't work out today. You will be able to see him in two weeks. Isn't that when you are scheduled to visit with him?" and hung up. He called back. George answered and said, "Who the hell do you think you are?" before hanging up on him.

Elliott called the police. He told them he now had a court order, and although it was vague, it did say that he had visiting time that afternoon. Elliot drove to Jean's house, followed by a patrol car. Elliot and the officer knocked on the door.

George answered the door and said Jean was ill from stress and couldn't talk with them. He said Jack was also ill and didn't want to visit with Elliott. The police insisted, and eventually Jean came to the door carrying a sleepy, tearful Jack. Jean told the police Jack didn't want to see Elliott and said to Jack, "Tell the nice policeman what you told me."

Jack said, "No see him."

Jean told the police Elliott might have been abusing Jack and had "made no effort in any way, shape, or form" to see Jack since the separation.

She further noted that Jack now called George "Daddy," and she didn't want to confuse him with two daddies. She said Elliott had driven her out of the house with physical and verbal abuse. To bolster her argument, she played back Elliott's last message, which was completely lacking in civility.

Elliott insisted on his visitation time, and the officer agreed. Jean said, "Okay, if that is what you want," closed the door, and returned fifteen minutes later with a very unhappy child who was saying that he didn't want to leave his mother and that he "hate[d] Elliott." His father picked him up and put him in his car, and they drove home.

On the way home, Jack's mood quickly improved. He responded to his dad's questions, quickly began calling him "Dad," and seemed happy when they talked about going out to get pizza.

When they got home, Jack looked around, recognized his familiar home, became very "Momsick," and told his dad he wanted to see his mother. Elliott, no child development specialist, angrily said, "No, you are staying here. I have had it with your mother. She left me. I didn't leave her." Jack began crying and tried to open the front door to run back to his mom. Elliott grabbed Jack and said, "I've had all I am going to take. I am your father. If your mother hadn't shacked up with George, we would all still be living here. It is your mother's entire fault. Now shut up or I will give you something to cry about."

Jack settled down. They went out for pizza, played video games for a while, and then returned home and watched a movie Elliott had rented. By 10:00 p.m. Jack was very sleepy and went to bed. He was happy to be in his own bed. The next morning he appeared happy, ate a good breakfast, and started watching his favorite television show. He then grew pensive and said he wanted to see his mother. Elliott relented and took Jack to Jean's house two hours before the scheduled exchange time.

The following week, Elliott received yet another declaration in which Jean said he had returned Jack early because he was unable to control him. Further, according to Jack, Elliott had called her bad names. She asked that all visitations be stopped.

The following were some of the difficulties experienced by Jack's family:

- Forming a new relationship before completing an old one
- Fantasizing a perfect mate
- Rushing into separation
- Not obtaining a temporary parenting order immediately
- Being a malicious parent
- Allowing interference by a significant other
- Making false accusations about a parent
- Not observing new boundaries
- Exaggerating declaration claims
- Not honoring an agreement
- Forcing compliance to a parenting plan with the child nearby
- Attempting to alienate a child from a parent
- Introducing a new partner to the child too quickly

# PART 3

---

# Co-parent Communication

Learning to communicate, parent to parent, is one of the most important things you can do for your child. There are three parts to effective co-parent communication: the Information Call, the Weekly Co-parenting Call, and the Semiyearly Meeting.

# CHAPTER 14

---

# The Information Call

We have talked about the child's paradox and co-parent paranoia, and the very negative effect they have on your child. They are harmful and result in distorted communication and are the major reason parents call each other liars. There are several things you can do to lessen the paradox and the paranoia for your child:

- Work to establish a co-parenting arrangement that is business-like and mutually respectful.
- Do not fight in front of your child.
- Reassure your child frequently that it is okay to love both parents.
- Never use exchange time to discuss co-parenting issues.

## The Information Call

The Information Call is made as needed, covering only one subject, within twenty-four hours of the event. It is a time-limited call. It is not the time for lengthy discussions about your child. The Semiyearly Meeting and the Weekly Co-Parent Call will be used for that purpose. The information call has two purposes:

1. To exchange urgent information that cannot wait until the next scheduled co-parent telephone call. This call provides parents with the opportunity to discuss unscheduled events, such as unplanned school activities or emergency medical care.

2. To coordinate co-parenting to handle unusual situations that arise out of information provided by a child. A child will often tell a parent something that appears to be of importance, but additional information is needed from the other parent to appropriately discuss the issue with the child.

## Making an Information Call

- Call the other parent and begin, "This is an information call." By doing so, you are signaling to the other parent that the call is to exchange one piece of information and is important. It lets the other parent know that you are going to talk about one subject and not try to persuade the other parent to change.

- You then give the information briefly but completely. For example, you might say, "Johnny's teacher just called. Johnny and most of the second grade have lice. I have a list of instructions that the teacher has asked us to follow, including some medication. If you wish, I will get the medicine and bring it over to you with written instructions."

- The other parent repeats back the information, clears up any misunderstanding, and terminates the call. The parent may say, "I will be home at five; could you bring the medicine then?"

- Neither parent uses this opportunity to blame the other parent. The task is simply to follow the instructions and get Johnny free from lice.

- Neither parent can bring up another subject. Often when parents do talk, they have so many issues they need to discuss that they try to cover them all in one telephone call. This simply leads to confusion and misunderstanding.

- Any further discussion about the lice situation can be covered during the weekly telephone call.

## A Call to Coordinate Shared Parenting

When parents have separated and are not talking with each other, their child often becomes the conduit of information. Each parent will hear things from the child that need to be clarified.

For example, little Karla overheard her father Bob talking to his new girlfriend. He had said Karla's mother was a "slut." Karla was playing by herself, unnoticed by either her father or his girlfriend.

When she was next at her mother's home, she was somewhat pensive and withdrawn. Just before going to bed, she said, "Mommy, what is a slot?"

Her mother became very angry and was further convinced that Bob was trying to alienate Karla from her. She was tempted to tell Karla that her father was wrong, as usual, but chose to make an information call.

In cases such as this, call the other parent and say, "This is an information call," preparing the way for a no-fault, nondefensive exchange of information. The parent states exactly what the child said and then waits for the other parent to respond. The calling parent doesn't rant, rave, accuse, or threaten. That would cut off any chance of communicating. The purpose is simply to exchange information.

## Mom Made an Information Call

"Hi, Bob. This is Nancy. Karla just asked me, 'Mommy, what is a slot?' Then she said you had called me a slot. I finally figured out she meant 'slut' and told Karla that it was a word people sometimes said when they were angry."

The parent who has been asked for information has several options at this point:

- Tell a lie. However, this means the parent is lying to the child too because the other parent will go back to the child to discuss the issue.
- Tell the truth. If a parent is saying such things around the child, he or she can now admit it and work to change.
- Reply that he or she has no idea where the statement came from. If the parent sincerely does not know where the statement came

from, he or she should say so. The other parent probably won't believe that at first, but if information calls are made when needed, a foundation for a business-like trust can be developed.

- Tell a kernel of truth. Recall an event that occurred that the child might have misconstrued or a conversation the child accidentally overheard.

Upon hearing the parent's response, the calling parent says thank you, terminates the telephone call, talks to the child, and discusses the issue with the other parent during the next weekly telephone call.

In this case, Bob was quite flustered. He had called Nancy a slut while talking to his girlfriend, and although he'd known Karla was nearby, he hadn't thought she had heard. Finally he said, "Jeez. I guess I might have, but I didn't know she was listening. I'll be more careful."

Note to all parents: A basic law of child development is that a child may not hear the words "go to bed," even if spoken loudly three feet away, but if in the same neighborhood the child will hear one parent make a negative comment about the other. So watch it!

Here, Nancy said, "Thank you" and terminated the telephone call. She then talked with Karla. "You know, sometimes parents say mean things when they are angry. I talked with Dad, and he said he was angry, talking with Kendra, and didn't know you were listening. He said he wouldn't say bad things about me again."

Following is another example of an information call that emphasizes the importance of parents communicating as co-parents. Children view their parents as very powerful and will use what they say to get what they want.

One Thursday afternoon after arriving at his father's home for the weekend, Chris told his Dad, "Mom says I don't have to go to school tomorrow." Dad became very angry, thinking Chris's mother was trying to control him again and alienate him from his son.

He told their SPSP therapist, "I hate it when she does that. She says things like that to Chris so I have to tell him to go to school; then he thinks I am the bad guy."

## We Practiced the Information Call

Dad called Chris's mom and said, "Hello, this is an information call. Chris just told me you told him he didn't have to go to school tomorrow."

Mom thought for a minute and said, "I have no idea. Wait! I do know. This morning he had a slight fever, and I mentioned to him that if it got worse, he would miss school."

"Thank you. He seems to be okay now," Dad said and terminated the call. He then took Chris's temperature, ready to make a simple decision: if Chris had a temperature, he would stay home; if he didn't, he would go to school.

This could have been an honest mistake on Chris's part, or he could have been trying to take advantage of his parents' refusal to talk with each other. Or Mom could have been trying to manipulate Dad. But now Chris knew his parents were starting to communicate. He could feel safer, knowing his parents were talking about his best interests, even if it reduced his chance to manipulate his parents.

Practice making a few information calls. You may find that it is easy to lapse into blaming or arguing, but over time you will learn how to talk with each other, exchange needed information, give your children a sense of parental unity, and provide positive co-parenting.

I suggest that you keep a record of the calls you make, at least for a while. You can look back over your notes and see if a theme emerges and if you are able to keep defensiveness at a minimum. In the back of the book is a form you can copy so that you can keep a record of your information calls.

If you make information calls and develop effective co-parent communication, you will have passed the greatest risk divorced parents face: believing your child is always telling the truth and believing the other parent is always lying. Once you practice this skill, many of your co-parent conflicts will disappear, and your child will be one step closer to adjusting to the divorce.

# CHAPTER 15

<hr>

## The Weekly Co-parenting Call

The Weekly Co-parenting Call is the mainstay of the communication system. It is the regularly scheduled call when you communicate as co-parents about the needs of your child.

By following this business-like communication system, you will have ample opportunity to discuss your child and not have to worry about "the right time" or the right number of times to call the other parent. You will not have to worry about intrusions on your time by the other parent.

You can stay focused on the needs of your child, following a precise agenda using the Co-parent Checklist found at the end of this chapter. As you grow accustomed to making the weekly co-parent call, you can communicate more effectively and feel more comfortable that a clear avenue of communication has been established.

### How to Make the Weekly Co-parent Call

- Select a day and time to call every week. Work out a time when each parent will have fifteen minutes away from any distractions, without the child close by, to go through the Co-parent Checklist.

- The value of picking a time for the Weekly Co-parent Call and sticking with it is great. Even if parents are going through a conflicted period, they know that at a certain time each week, they will be communicating regarding their child.

- Parents should discuss the child with their new partner before making the call, but the new partner should not be present when the call is made.

- Parents will alternate making the call.

- The person making the call then "chairs" the meeting, either discussing the item first or having the other parent initiate the discussion. If one parent has rated the item as a "5," meaning no problem, and the other parent rates it as "1," meaning a serious problem, it is better to listen first to the parent who is saying there is a major problem.

- Do not skip to problem areas. As you make calls, you will find there are fewer and fewer problems. When you separated, about all that was left were the impasse issues. Now it is important to talk about and reinforce your good co-parenting skills. For example, if you had a major issue with school, but worked together and school is now going well, be sure to mention the item each time. Many parents use a shorthand: "That's a five." Just remember that means, "We are doing well as co-parents."

- The goal is to inform, not to persuade.

- You can briefly discuss an issue on which you hold a difference of opinion. If you can come to a decision quickly, do so. If not, then arrange to make a call to discuss this single item, setting a limit of thirty minutes. If you can't make a decision by then, have a mediator help you do so.

- Over time your ratings on most areas will move toward a five. A few will remain as problems. Review the problem issue each week, attempting to rephrase the problem. Often the solution to a problem is in asking the right question.

- Keep a record of all decisions you make.

- If you feel overwhelmed, say so, hang up, and make the next regularly scheduled call the next week.

- If you continue making the calls, you will lose your sense of urgency and be able to relax, knowing that all humans have differences, and if you have a problem that is hard to resolve, you are just being human.
- Make as many copies of the Co-parent Checklist as you want.

## Jim and Harriet Were Furious but Never Lost Face

Jim and Harriet struggled through a ten-year relationship before deciding to divorce. By then they had a daughter, Barbara, age eight. They were chronically incompatible. Harriet's parents were military, but she rebelled against their authority very early. She knew how to clean house, cook, and take care of the household expenses but chose a less structured way of life. Jim's parents were also military. After a brief rebellious period during college, he settled down and enjoyed a highly structured life.

Neither was able to accept the other, buying into the refrain, "If only he/she would change, everything would be all right." They sought couples' counseling with a counselor who wanted them to look each other in the eye and say, "I love you." Harriet found this meaningful, but for Jim, it just didn't add up.

They divorced, and their anger overwhelmed them.

Their anger increased, their communication decreased, and each became convinced that the other parent was totally at fault.

When they were together, their decision-making process was one of their impasse issues. Jim wanted hard data. He wanted a timetable. He wanted decisions made in a timely manner. Harriet wanted to think about each issue, decide how she felt, and sooner or later make a decision.

Fortunately, they were referred to the Shared Parenting Support Program by their attorneys and were able to work to keep boundaries clear. For example, Jim could not tell her how to clean house. Harriet could not tell him how to raise their daughter.

They made co-parenting decisions slowly, but came to realize that they were at least once again making decisions. They decided to make their weekly co-parent telephone call at 3:00 p.m. on Fridays. They reasoned that Barbara got out of school at 3:45 and moved from one home to the other on Friday. They could exchange information just before she made the transfer to the other parent.

They made an occasional information call. They met with their SPSP therapist for a semiyearly meeting. They had been making weekly co-parent telephone calls for the past six months. They were moving through the difficult post-divorce adjustment and were finding they could co-parent successfully.

Then one Wednesday, when Harriet was bringing Barbara to her father for a midweek dinner visit, Jim told Harriet, in front of Barbara, that he would be out of town the following week, during Harriet's parenting time, and she "had" to let him take Barbara with him. He was going to Los Angeles, his parents were going with him, and he would have time to take Barbara to Disneyland. Harriet, in front of Barbara, told him they were no longer married, and she didn't "have" to do anything he told her. The following week was her parenting time; he should have discussed it with her earlier, and besides, she didn't need to have a reason to say no. She slammed the door in Jim's face.

Barbara, of course, became very upset. She started crying and said, "Mommy, why not?" Harriet told her it was a grown-up problem, and she wouldn't understand. Barbara, of course, understood that her dream trip to Disneyland during regularly scheduled school time was in jeopardy. She spent the next day working on her mother. Harriet was livid. Jim had just reactivated all the old impasse issues—he had been smug, controlling, and thoughtless. She hated talking with him and felt very angry. Jim was upset, thinking Harriet would never change—she was being capricious, defiant, rebellious, and self-centered. They never wanted to talk with each other again.

However, both had some time to cool down and realized they were involved in a power struggle because of their old impasse issues. They realized they would be talking to each other Friday at 3:30, and each was trying to think of a way out of the stalemate without losing face. They both realized that it wasn't the parents' parenting time; it was Barbara's time to be with each parent. They realized that although it might be a grown-up problem, they were both acting very childishly.

On Friday, at 3:30 p.m., Jim called Harriet. "Hi, Harriet, time for our call." His words were polite, but his tone of voice let her know that he was still angry. She responded coolly. But they were talking.

Jim said, "I would like to talk about next week. I know you don't 'have' to, but I think Barbara would like a special trip like this. She has been working hard in school. In fact, I think she has been almost too good. I would like to reward her. My plan is to leave Monday after school and get her back to you by Thursday before school. What do you think?"

Harriet had listened carefully and didn't feel like she had to save face. Besides, upon reflection, she thought it would be a great trip for Barbara. "Well ... okay, but have her back for school on Thursday."

## A Successful Conclusion

Harriet and Jim were able to move past an old impasse issue. Barbara reported to her envious class that Mickey waved to her. The Weekly Co-parent Call assisted these well-meaning parents in moving past a difficult time in their efforts to successfully co-parent their daughter.

## The Co-parent Checklist

The following list contains the twenty essential co-parenting tasks. You can use this checklist to make a brief co-parent telephone call to assist you in your efforts to be effective co-parents.

## The Twenty Essential Co-parenting Tasks

*Make as many copies as you want*

5 = No problem, doing well; 1 = Major problem, proceed with caution

Circle for you, square for other parent

| | | | | | | |
|---|---|---|---|---|---|---|
| 1. | Alternative care | 1 | 2 | 3 | 4 | 5 |
| 2. | Behavior and discipline | 1 | 2 | 3 | 4 | 5 |
| 3. | Counseling and therapy | 1 | 2 | 3 | 4 | 5 |
| 4. | Clothing | 1 | 2 | 3 | 4 | 5 |
| 5. | Parent–parent–teacher cooperation | 1 | 2 | 3 | 4 | 5 |
| 6. | Giving your child an extended family | 1 | 2 | 3 | 4 | 5 |
| 7. | Extracurricular activities | 1 | 2 | 3 | 4 | 5 |
| 8. | Guiding your child's friendships | 1 | 2 | 3 | 4 | 5 |
| 9. | Hygiene | 1 | 2 | 3 | 4 | 5 |

| | | | | | | | |
|---|---|---|---|---|---|---|---|
| 10. | Teaching friends and relatives to behave | 1 | 2 | 3 | 4 | 5 |
| 11. | Providing medical and dental care | 1 | 2 | 3 | 4 | 5 |
| 12. | Values training | 1 | 2 | 3 | 4 | 5 |
| 13. | Parent–child telephone calls | 1 | 2 | 3 | 4 | 5 |
| 14. | Maintaining parent–child boundaries | 1 | 2 | 3 | 4 | 5 |
| 15. | Safety | 1 | 2 | 3 | 4 | 5 |
| 16. | Safe sexual development | 1 | 2 | 3 | 4 | 5 |
| 17. | Transportation | 1 | 2 | 3 | 4 | 5 |
| 18. | Peaceful exchanges | 1 | 2 | 3 | 4 | 5 |
| 19. | Vacation and holiday planning | 1 | 2 | 3 | 4 | 5 |
| 20. | Problem solving and crisis control | 1 | 2 | 3 | 4 | 5 |

# CHAPTER 16

---

# The Semiyearly Meeting

To be effective co-parents, meet on a regular basis for long-range planning. Without these meetings, your child may miss out on important activities. By not meeting to discuss your child's long-range needs, you are increasing the possibility of parental conflict, and important holidays can be marred by unintentional misunderstandings.

## The Long-Term Executive Session

The Semiyearly meeting is a one-hour executive meeting in which parents and stepparents meet together to structure the next six months of their child's life. By conducting these meetings, you are able to develop a sense of continuity and avoid many pitfalls of co-parenting.

## Meetings Are Held to Accommodate School Schedules

The semiyearly meetings are usually held in February and August if your child attends a traditional school. Parents of children attending year-round school may meet three times a year, accommodating the school schedule. Some parents are able to meet together at a coffee shop. Others feel more comfortable meeting with an SPSP therapist.

## The Entire Parenting Team Must Meet

It is necessary for stepparents and significant others to attend as well. Later in this chapter, you will find a form you can use for the semiyearly meeting. When you are preparing for the meeting, gather as much information as you can about vacation plans, schooling, holidays, and extracurricular activities. Bring your calendars.

## Confirming the Holiday and Vacation Schedules

Maintaining a schedule of holidays is a difficult task for an intact family. It is even more difficult for a two-home family. Many parents discover, at the very worst time, shortly before a holiday, that they disagree as to what the schedule will be. Consider the plight of Clint:

Clint and Dorothy planned to fly to Hawaii for Christmas, taking her two children and his two children with them. They planned ahead, buying the cheapest tickets they could find. The tickets were not refundable.

Clint and his ex-wife, Amanda, rarely talked. They had worked out an arrangement to exchange the children at school. The only times they saw each other were during exchanges when school was not in session. Their court order stated that Clint would have the children the first week of Christmas vacation on the odd years. Since their separation and divorce, four years earlier, the plan had worked fairly well. Neither parent looked at the custody plan, each having committed it to memory. Then one year, the week before the Christmas vacation was to start, one of their children, Claude, told his mom they were going to stay in a condo in Hawaii. Amanda assumed Clint and his new family were going to Hawaii the second half of the Christmas vacation.

Two days before school was out, Claude told his mom, "I can hardly wait to go to Hawaii on Saturday!" Amanda finally became aware that something was wrong and was torn between trying to figure out what was happening and letting Clint continue to believe he had the first week of the vacation. She decided to call him, reminding him that it was a year in which he would have the second half of the vacation. He became extremely angry, yelling at Amanda that she was once again trying to cause trouble. She somewhat enjoyed his anger, knowing that she was right, having read the parenting agreement just to make sure. She told him she and her husband had already made plans for Christmas with the children, and it "would not be possible" for him to have them the first week of the vacation. Clint, of course, threatened to take her to court. She said, "Read the agreement!" and terminated the call. They had been to court seven times, and those words, "I'll see you in court," brought back all the anger, hurt, and resentment they had experienced when separating. Clint read the agreement and discovered he was wrong. After composing himself, he called back. He had just spent several thousand dollars on nonrefundable tickets. He asked Amanda if she would be willing to trade vacation times at the last minute. She said, "Why should I, after the way you yelled at me and threatened to take me to court?" They argued. This time he terminated the call abruptly.

Fortunately, Amanda's husband, Clark, was not caught up in the conflict and pointed out to his wife that the kids were eager to go to Hawaii, and in the absence of major plans, perhaps she could accede to Clint's requests. He suggested Clint put in writing that Amanda would have the first week of the Christmas vacation the next year, and the year after they would return to their agreed-upon schedule.

The issue was resolved. Clint and his family were able to go to Hawaii, and Amanda still had a week's vacation with the children when they returned.

In many cases, the ending is not so happy. In this case the stepfather was able to perform his role very well; he was less emotionally involved and proposed a positive solution. But what would have happened if their mom also had purchased nonrefundable tickets and was not willing to give up her time? Then the court order would have been followed. Because of such misunderstandings, it is important to review the court order at the February meeting and the August meeting. Go over each holiday and confirm the schedule.

## Confirming the School Schedule

During the semiyearly meeting, review the school schedule. Don't take for granted that either of you know about every activity. It is important for both parents—and stepparents as well—to have the opportunity to attend open houses, plays, and teacher conferences. The object is to use all your resources to ensure your child gets the best possible education. If either parent has school schedules that the other does not have, make sure a copy is made. Nothing starts a fight as quickly as when a parent feels the other parent is withholding school information.

## Arranging Extracurricular Activities

I have known children who did not take part in sports or other activities because their parents were still locked in a power struggle or simply refused to talk with each other.

During the semiyearly meeting, parents can make decisions regarding extracurricular activities so that both parents are involved and committed.

Making co-parenting decisions is often very time-consuming. You may have very strong feelings about your child's involvement in a particular sport. One mother told me that she was a world-class swimmer and wanted her child to be on a team. The father, either for real reasons or just to be difficult, would not agree to cooperate in the swim program or permit the mother to take the child during his time to practice sessions. She was very disappointed, but an important boundary issue was at stake. The mother could have taken her child to practice every other week, but he would never really feel part of the team. She could not force the father to participate. As a result her child could not participate in team swimming. The child was involved in other activities, so there was not deprivation. Although one could argue that the father could have accommodated the mother's desire to have their child be on the swim team, he was not obligated to do so.

Sometimes life is just not fair. And there is nothing in the Ten Commandments or the Constitution that makes it immoral or illegal to be a jerk. A last resort for the mother would have been to pay for mediation of that one issue.

## Confirming Birthdays

Parents differ on the importance placed on birthdays. Some parents, for religious reasons, do not celebrate birthdays. Other parents feel that a birthday is a major event and make elaborate plans. Some stepparents place great importance on birthdays, wanting their own birthday to be celebrated and to be included in the celebration of the birthdays of their stepchildren. During the semiyearly meeting, make sure you understand the arrangement for the child's birthday and for each parent's birthday.

Whatever decisions you make during the semiyearly meeting must be put in writing. Each parent writes down what the agreement was and gives a copy to the other parent. You will find that sometimes your understanding of the agreement does not match that of the other parent. That doesn't mean you are a poor communicator. It just means that communicating with an ex-spouse is difficult, and emotions interfere with effective communication. It is better to check twice and confirm your agreement.

## Meeting the Changing Needs of Your Child

During the semiyearly meetings, you can discuss general questions regarding the welfare of your child. Is your child happy? Does he need more activities? Is she in the right school? Should he be in an accelerated learning program? Are both parents satisfied with her religious and moral training? Are his needs being met appropriately? Are parents spending about the same on presents and special rewards? Are parents able to focus on the needs of the child to minimize the impact of living in two homes?

A child's needs change over time. Court orders are usually written in stone. At each developmental age, the needs of your child will change. Effective co-parents will discuss these changes during their weekly co-parent telephone call and at their semiyearly meeting, making sure their child has a solid foundation of love and consistency and avoiding co-parent conflict as much as possible.

Copies of the February and August meeting forms are included here as well as in the epilogue. Make more copies if you wish.

## Agenda for Semiyearly Meeting

### February

Meeting location _____ Date _____

Lincoln's/MLK's Birthday _____

_____

Presidents Day _____

_____

Passover _____

_____

Easter _____

_____

Spring Break _____

_____

Mother's Day _____

_____

Memorial Day _____

_____

Father's Day _____

_____

Independence Day _____

_____

Formal vacations _____

_____

Birthdays _____

_____

_____

_____

_____

Other _____

_____

Extracurricular _____

School activities _____

_____

_____

Assessment of child and need for action (education, social, rules, happiness,

and morals) _____

_____

_____

Decisions made during this semiyearly meeting _____

_____

_____

_____

_____

_____

_____

_____

## Agenda for Semiyearly Meeting

## August

Location _____ Date _____

Labor Day _____

_____

Columbus Day _____

_____

Halloween _____

_____

Veterans Day _____

_____

Thanksgiving _____

_____

Chanukah _____

_____

Christmas Vacation _____

_____

Christmas Eve/Day _____

_____

New Year's _____

_____

Formal vacations _____

_____

Birthdays _____

_____

_____

_____

_____

_____

Other _____

Extracurricular _____

_____

_____

_____

School activities _____

_____

_____

_____

_____

Assessment of child and need for action (education, social, rules, happiness, and morals) _____

_____

_____

Decisions made during this semiyearly meeting _____

_____

_____

_____

_____

_____

_____

_____

# PART 4

---

# The Twenty Essential
# Co-parenting Tasks

The last step is to put your agreements to work. There are only twenty tasks that most parents who raise their child in two homes must learn. Divorce is in the details.

# CHAPTER 17

⸻ ◆ ⸻

# Selecting and Maintaining
# Alternative Care Providers

"Alternative care" refers to all care providers other than parents, stepparents, or school. It includes all sitters, day care providers, and relatives or friends who provide care for your child. Selecting alternative care providers is an important task for parents, divorced or not. It becomes even more crucial when parents are raising their child in two homes. The following is a case in point.

Margaret provided care for two children in her home from after school until the children's parents picked them up after work. One of the children, Betsy, seemed to have asthma. For some reason, parents argue about asthma. One parent may be concerned, having had asthma as a child. The other parent may believe that the child is fine and that all that medical attention will only make the child a hypochondriac. Betsy's mom had suffered from asthma as a child and was aware of how claustrophobic it could feel when a person is unable to take a deep breath. Betsy's dad was a rugged outdoor type who avoided medication whenever possible. When Betsy's breathing was ragged, he would say to her, "All you have to do is stand up straight and get more exercise. You will be fine."

Betsy's pediatrician saw her and prescribed an inhaler. He noted that Betsy had a minor asthma problem, which seemed to be worse after school, in the late afternoon. He said it would be best for Betsy to use the inhaler, with adult supervision, if she felt shortness of breath. Mom talked to Margaret, explaining the doctor's order and giving her an inhaler to use. Dad independently talked with the pediatrician (susceptible to the pediatrician paradox) and confirmed that Betsy's condition was not life-threatening, and Betsy would not suffer enduring harm if not given the inhaler. Dad told Margaret, "Dr. Smith said Betsy was all right. I am concerned with children being overmedicated. Betsy really doesn't need the inhaler, and I would not want to see her made dependent on medication."

Margaret, caught in the care provider paradox, used a technique many children use: she led two lives. When Mom was to pick up Betsy after work, Margaret was more likely to let Betsy use the inhaler if she had difficulty breathing. When Dad was to pick her up, Margaret was more likely to not give Betsy the inhaler and tell her to rest for a few minutes.

Betsy solved the problem of the pediatrician/day care provider/child paradox by hiding the fact that at times she felt short of breath. Dad felt vindicated since she never asked for medication.

## Selecting and Maintaining Alternative Care Providers

In selecting and maintaining care providers, the purpose is to provide a consistent environment for your child. Children of divorce experience more changes in their lives than they can comfortably accept. Where they spend time, other than home and school, is no exception. The fewer changes you make for your child, the easier he or she can adapt to the environment.

A parent is most often the first choice to care for your child. Parents often struggle over this issue. Mom may work from nine to five and Dad from six to two. The child may go to school from eight to two. Common sense suggests that Mom should take the child to school, and Dad should provide after-school care. Sometimes a parent will argue that permitting the nonresidential parent to provide after-school care is an intrusion. It is an intrusion only on the parents. The primary issue is: what is best for the child? An arrangement in which the nonresidential parent provides care daily will result in almost daily contact between parents. Whether they will be able to handle it is the question.

Use day care to provide needed socialization. Some parents determine that their child needs more time with other children to provide social training and structure. Even if parents can work together and provide all the care needed, they may decide that two afternoons a week in day care would be a positive experience.

Select care providers acceptable to both parents. Parents need to agree on who will provide care for their child. Some decisions are obvious: a mature, responsible, warm, competent adult is preferred. A person with a criminal record or history of drug usage or who has molested or abused children, is too old and infirm, or is too young and immature should be ruled out by both parents. Sometimes a parent will reject a caretaker out of anger or past grievance rather than for a realistic reason. For example, a grandmother may be a highly qualified caretaker but in conflict with one of the child's parents. It is time for the parents to reconcile with the extended family.

A parent may select an inappropriate caregiver and then accuse the other parent of being "unreasonable." It is generally best to let the parent's veto stand and use alternative providers.

If an outside caretaker is needed, it is usually better to use a person who is licensed. That does not guarantee the person is without negative qualities, but it lessens the chance, since in most jurisdictions, persons applying for licensure will have had a background check.

If needed, parents can enlist the help of a mediator to evaluate the proposed alternative caregiver. If one parent rejects all potential care providers, it should be obvious that the parent is obstructing effective co-parenting or the other parent is very poor at selecting care providers. Return to mediation. Discuss the issue with an attorney. Be specific about the issue.

It is in the Co-parent's Bill of Rights and Responsibilities (see Appendix F) that each parent must have sufficient information about persons who have contact with the children. Effective co-parenting means keeping the other parent informed. If a new caretaker is to be used, discuss this with the other parent and let the other parent know before the caretaker starts. Provide in-depth information about the proposed caretaker. It is not appropriate to say, "She is my new girlfriend, and she is okay." The parent must provide information such as name, address, telephone number, occupation, schooling, motivation to provide care, qualities that make the person "okay" and any drawbacks as caretaker.

Give care providers the opportunity to do their best, unencumbered by the care provider's paradox. Persons who take care of your child have the same needs as anyone else: to be liked, to be loyal, and to be trusted. If parents are warring and give conflicting information to the care provider, that person may attempt to solve the paradox using some of the same unworkable skills as your child. Some day care providers, faced with contradictory demands, may act as though agreeing with both parents. The problem can be as minor as what after-school treat to give the child to as major as administering proper medication.

Whether there are one or two day care providers, and whether the provider is Mom, Dad, Grandma, the next-door neighbor, or a licensed professional hired with references, parents need to discuss and agree on a set of guidelines. It is detrimental to disagree and place the disagreement in the hands of the provider. If parents disagree and cannot reach agreement through discussion, then they should take the issue to a mediator.

Areas of agreement for the care provider:

- Nap time or not
- When to take a nap
- Toilet training issues
- Medication for the child
- What to do if the child acts up
- What to do if the parent is unavoidably late
- What to do if the child becomes ill or is injured
- What foods the child can/cannot eat
- Whether the child should do homework or not at the day care provider's home

- How much, if any, TV the child can watch
- Who can/cannot call the child
- Who the backup persons are in case of a parent emergency
- What to do if a parent chronically changes rules and schedule

# CHAPTER 18

---

# Socialization and Discipline

It is possible for divorced parents to teach their children how to become effective, responsible citizens by working together; providing a loving, pleasant structure; and setting realistic, growth-producing limits and normal, natural consequences to behavior. When there are big differences between parenting styles, it is even more important for parents to establish a set of rules and provide a consistent environment for their child.

Most of what a child learns in life is learned willingly and eagerly, with a desire to please. Many of the tasks of growing up are hardwired into our system, such as the desire to laugh, crawl, walk, eat, eliminate, sleep, play, and be part of a group. It is the parents' job to teach their child the everyday rules of living. Some children seem to learn the rules of living easily; others have the need to test these rules. Our culture is riddled with concepts of "discipline" and "punishment." Teaching a child the rules of successful living rarely requires praise or punishment. Children have an innate desire to learn, to be part of a family, to be part of a group, and to be happy. If parents trust that children have these built-in needs, their job becomes easier. With careful help children learn how to get along in a complex world, to balance individual needs with the needs of the group, and to be useful, productive, reasonably happy adults.

## Never Ask Your Child to Do Something a Dead Person Can Do

Children are filled with life and have a built-in need to walk, talk, run, explore, taste, listen, and feel. If you tell your child to "be quiet," you are asking for something a dead person can do. Rather, ask your child to do something befitting a life, a human child. Rather than say, "Be quiet," say, "Come here and whisper what you want me to know."

One illustration I heard has stuck with me. A small child who'd had a hard life was finally with a family that understood the principle of how to talk to live children. The child spilled a glass of milk on the table. During the hard period of his life, he would have been yelled at and hit. The new father said "Quick, let's lap it up!" thus giving the child a lifetime memory and a story to illustrate positive parenting.

## It Is Always a Matter of Finding a Balance

Some parents are too lenient, permitting their child to become a self-focused little monster. Other parents become too punitive, resulting in an overly controlled, resentful, worried child. Still other parents are inconsistent, resulting in a confused, overly self-sufficient, or delinquent child. What we need to teach our children is that there are rules of living in our society that bring positive results.

Parenting is a cooperative effort. Whether as part of an intact family or a family living in two homes, parents must share the responsibility of socializing their child. Parents, like cops, will alternate being the occasional bad guy. Parents will also share in providing the rewards. The child's good life must be worth preserving. When a child feels life is hopeless, there is little one can do to "punish" and little good behavior that can be rewarded. The loss of hope is an evil thing.

## The 51 Percent Theory

If life does not provide at least 51 percent pleasure over 49 percent pain, any one of us may rebel.

Abby and Joe struggled with the question of how much praise to use to encourage positive behavior and how much pain to stop unwanted behavior.

Neither Abby nor Joe had been mistreated as a child, but coming from strict families, they had been expected to behave. If they did not behave, they were swatted, usually by the mother, or spanked, usually by the father. When they became parents, they "knew" they would not spank their daughter. They had courses in child behavior and "knew" that love would prevail. However, they did not know, until they experienced it, that a two-year-old will sometimes not want to (a) stand, (b) sit, (c) lie down, or (d) be held. It was very tempting to give their daughter Aretha a "quick swat." They reasoned, "This child is totally impossible. My parents swatted me, and I turned out sort of okay. One quick swat and …" Of course, Aretha screamed louder, which led Abby and Joe to say, "If you keep this up, I'll give you something to cry about." With the help of a friend (who happened to be a very sensible child psychologist), they evaluated what they were doing. Sometimes kids cry for no apparent reason. Giving them "something to cry about" is a form of insanity.

Sometimes there is nothing a parent can do except tolerate the child's discontent. Of course, that is what we do with our grown-up friends. Imagine you are talking to a friend who tells you, "I've about had it. I have never been so down. I could really cry." If you follow punitive child-rearing practices, you might say, "I'll give you something to feel depressed about," and hit the offending adult with a paddle. Rather than give Aretha something to cry about, her parents could make sure she wasn't in danger, take her away from places that would disturb other people, and make her feel safe and secure until the storm passed.

One consolation for parents who want to do the right thing: Justice Learned Hand said even a dog knows the difference between being tripped over and being kicked. So does your kid, who will forgive you for all sorts of trespasses if you trespassed doing the best you could, without cruelty.

## Socialization: A Cooperative Venture between You and Your Child

Children are eager to learn and gain your approval. Only a small percent of their training to be adults comes in the form of discipline. Punishment, whether verbal, physical, or through body language, can stop unwanted behavior. Praise and rewards will start and help continue wanted behavior. If your child receives clear, simple messages, little discipline is needed. To stop a child from running in the street and being run over, most parents will yell, "Stop!" And some will swat the child. Most will simply hold the childs hand snugly until the age of reason. Running in the street is a behavior to be stopped.

To increase the frequency with which a child says "thank you," most parents will say, "You are welcome," or in other ways acknowledge the child's worth.

Children (and adults) can learn only if the consequences are consistent. If you spank for swearing one time and laugh another time, or if you yourself swear, your child is left with the decision of whether or not to swear.

It is best if divorced parents and stepparents do not hit the child. It only alienates the child and will make the adults vulnerable to accusations of abuse. Parents should share with each other the socialization styles.

# CHAPTER 19

---

## Counseling and Therapy

As parents, you can assess your own level of stress and seek help if you wish. Sometimes it is more difficult to decide whether your child needs counseling. By discussing the issue with the other parent, you can arrive at an informed decision about your child's need for therapy. Here are some guidelines you may find helpful.

- Don't select a therapist who has seen you or the other parent. Some therapists will accept more than one family member for individual treatment, but it is not appropriate, creating a conflict of interest.
- Always gain the cooperation of the other parent before involving your child in therapy.
- Insist that your child's therapist does not become involved in the legal battle.
- If a parent has already taken the child to a therapist without the other parent's consent, parents should seek help to determine whether they should continue treatment with that therapist, change to a different therapist, or terminate therapy.

- Parents must decide (a) what symptoms the child is showing that require therapeutic intervention and (b) what therapist the child should see.
- A child's involvement in therapy should be made rationally, without anyone taking the extreme positions that "therapy is always harmful" or "therapy is always needed."
- If your child's therapist finds evidence of physical, emotional, or sexual abuse, it will be reported to the proper authorities. Listen carefully, be open and honest, and don't jump to conclusions. Therapists are required to report suspicions of abuse.

Use the following form as a way to objectively discuss your child's needs.

## Child Behavior Checklist

Rate your child's behavior: 1 = major problem; 5 = doing well.

| Behavior | Parents' Ratings | Mother and Father | Total |
|---|---|---|---|
| Argumentative | 1 2 3 4 5 | _____ | |
| Bullies others | 1 2 3 4 5 | _____ | |
| Disobedient | 1 2 3 4 5 | _____ | |
| Stubborn | 1 2 3 4 5 | _____ | |
| Teases others | 1 2 3 4 5 | _____ | |
| DOMINANT BEHAVIOR | | | _____ |
| | | | |
| Withdrawn | 1 2 3 4 5 | _____ | |
| Lacks energy | 1 2 3 4 5 | _____ | |
| Stares blankly | 1 2 3 4 5 | _____ | |
| Secretive | 1 2 3 4 5 | _____ | |
| Refuses to talk | 1 2 3 4 5 | _____ | |
| WITHDRAWING BEHAVIOR | | | _____ |
| | | | |
| Steals | 1 2 3 4 5 | _____ | |
| Cheats | 1 2 3 4 5 | _____ | |
| Runs away | 1 2 3 4 5 | _____ | |
| Lies | 1 2 3 4 5 | _____ | |
| Bad friends | 1 2 3 4 5 | _____ | |
| ANTISOCIAL BEHAVIOR | | | _____ |
| | | | |
| Aches and pains | 1 2 3 4 5 | _____ | |
| Headaches | 1 2 3 4 5 | _____ | |
| Sickly | 1 2 3 4 5 | _____ | |
| Stomach aches | 1 2 3 4 5 | _____ | |
| Nausea | 1 2 3 4 5 | _____ | |
| ACHES AND PAINS | | | _____ |

| | | | | | | |
|---|---|---|---|---|---|---|
| Anxious | 1 | 2 | 3 | 4 | 5 | _____ |
| Fearful | 1 | 2 | 3 | 4 | 5 | _____ |
| Low self-esteem | 1 | 2 | 3 | 4 | 5 | _____ |
| Sad, depressed | 1 | 2 | 3 | 4 | 5 | _____ |
| Worries a lot | 1 | 2 | 3 | 4 | 5 | _____ |
| DEPRESSION | | | | | | _____ |

| | | | | | | |
|---|---|---|---|---|---|---|
| Stays awake | 1 | 2 | 3 | 4 | 5 | _____ |
| Bad dreams | 1 | 2 | 3 | 4 | 5 | _____ |
| Wets bed | 1 | 2 | 3 | 4 | 5 | _____ |
| Sleeps too much | 1 | 2 | 3 | 4 | 5 | _____ |
| Wakes too early | 1 | 2 | 3 | 4 | 5 | _____ |
| SLEEP ADJUSTMENT | | | | | | _____ |

| | | | | | | |
|---|---|---|---|---|---|---|
| Picky eater | 1 | 2 | 3 | 4 | 5 | _____ |
| Overeater | 1 | 2 | 3 | 4 | 5 | _____ |
| Junk food preference | 1 | 2 | 3 | 4 | 5 | _____ |
| Resists new foods | 1 | 2 | 3 | 4 | 5 | _____ |
| Eats too little | 1 | 2 | 3 | 4 | 5 | _____ |
| EATING ADJUSTMENT | | | | | | _____ |

| | | | | | | |
|---|---|---|---|---|---|---|
| Teacher conflict | 1 | 2 | 3 | 4 | 5 | _____ |
| Peer conflict | 1 | 2 | 3 | 4 | 5 | _____ |
| Homework conflict | 1 | 2 | 3 | 4 | 5 | _____ |
| Grades below ability | 1 | 2 | 3 | 4 | 5 | _____ |
| Not motivated | 1 | 2 | 3 | 4 | 5 | _____ |
| SCHOOL ADJUSTMENT | | | | | | _____ |

| | | | | | | |
|---|---|---|---|---|---|---|
| Leaves things behind | 1 | 2 | 3 | 4 | 5 | _____ |
| Complains about plans | 1 | 2 | 3 | 4 | 5 | _____ |
| Angry at parent(s) | 1 | 2 | 3 | 4 | 5 | _____ |
| Resists exchange | 1 | 2 | 3 | 4 | 5 | _____ |
| Long adjustment time | 1 | 2 | 3 | 4 | 5 | _____ |

TRANSITION PROBLEMS _____

| | | | | | | |
|---|---|---|---|---|---|---|
| Loyalty conflicts | 1 | 2 | 3 | 4 | 5 | _____ |
| Guilt about divorce | 1 | 2 | 3 | 4 | 5 | _____ |
| Distant from parent(s) | 1 | 2 | 3 | 4 | 5 | _____ |
| Angry at both parents | 1 | 2 | 3 | 4 | 5 | _____ |
| Slow adjustment | 1 | 2 | 3 | 4 | 5 | _____ |

DIVORCE ADJUSTMENT _____

# CHAPTER 20

---

# Clothing

Nothing seems to vex divorced parents as much as keeping their child clothed. There is only one way to handle the issue of clothing for your child who lives in two homes: relax, lighten up, accept the responsibility of the two-home situation, and understand that the clothing belongs to the child. Following are guidelines for maintaining one or two wardrobes.

## If You Decide on One Wardrobe

- Decide how much is to be spent on clothing by means of child support.
- Decide whether "big-ticket" items, such as shoes and coats, are separate purchases and are to be paid for separately from the amount allocated in child support. Decide what to do when a big-ticket item is missing or lost.
- Decide who will actually purchase the clothing.
- Make sure your child is not involved in conflict over clothing.
- A child's self-esteem will rest on dressing like other children. Make your child feel good.

## If You Decide to Have Two Wardrobes

- Decide generally the price range of clothing that will be purchased. Avoid Salvation Army clothing at one home and custom-made clothing at the other.
- Decide what clothing the child will wear going from one home to the other.
- Decide what will happen to the exchange clothing at the receiving parent's home. It is not to be ridiculed and fumigated in the front yard. Wash it carefully and return it to the other parent.
- The responsibility for clothing in two-home families is the parents', not the child's. Parents must make sure the clothing is purchased within the financial structure of the parents, cleaned, and returned to the appropriate home.
- Children must never be included in arguments about clothing, money, or cleanliness. These are parenting issues.
- You may have bought the clothes, but they belong to your child—unless, of course, you have worked out a rental contract that can be read and signed by a two-year-old. Even so, most courts would not honor a contract signed by a two-year-old child.

# CHAPTER 21

---

# Parent–Parent–Teacher Cooperation

Selecting and supporting a school for your child is one of the more difficult tasks you will face as co-parents. It is one of the most visible tasks co-parents must share. When lives are disrupted by divorce, many changes occur within the family, including where each parent will live, the most appropriate and convenient school assignment for your child, and learning to co-parent so that the child's school experience is positive and growth producing.

The teacher's paradox is an important consideration. Some teachers may easily accommodate a divorced child. Others feel sympathy for the "unfortunate victim" of divorce and may try to compensate by overprotection. Other teachers have experienced the battle firsthand, listening to parents quarrel, receiving subpoenas to appear in court as a witness for either Mom or Dad, or being accused of favoring one parent or the other. Other teachers feel the differing demands of each parent and try to not take sides but unfortunately may give parents contradictory messages.

All aspects of managing your child's school experience can present problems, including selecting a school based on location, educational needs, proximity to each parent, and prior school history. As stepparents are added to the co-parenting team, the issue of division of duties becomes increasingly important.

## Nine Guidelines for School Success

By having advanced knowledge of the issues, you can make your child's school life more enjoyable and educational.

- Parents must agree on what type of school the child will attend. The choices are public, private, home schooling, and denominational. The decision must be made based on your child's needs as well as convenience for parents. If you agree on a solution that meets your child's needs and is also convenient, so much the better.

- As parents make the decisions about where to live, consider living in the same school district, more than two miles and less than seven miles apart. You will be able to maintain a proper boundary between homes, which is especially important when your child is older and can bicycle over a large area. But by living in the same district, you can all attend school activities and actively support your child's education.

- If you cannot decide on a school, you may need to hire a consultant, preferably a school psychologist or guidance counselor, to help you with the decision.

- Your child's wishes must be considered, but the final decision is one for parents to make. Stepparent views will be heard, but Mom and Dad make the final decisions.

- Once you decide on a school, you must decide on the logistics. How will your child get to and from school? Who will take care of enrollment? Should the entire executive group (parents and stepparents) attend each teacher's meeting? How can you best develop a positive relationship so that the executive team can attend all school activities to provide support for your child? Who will be available to take the child on field trips?

- Parents must then work together to determine a system to get current, up-to-date information from the school. Some schools will send duplicate information to each parent. Other schools prefer you make your own arrangements to exchange information. Whatever you do, don't pass messages through your child. What seems to work best is to have the teacher send a copy of school information to each parent. Each parent in turn sends a copy to the other parent. Although you may receive two or three copies of the schedule, that is better than not receiving a notice of some important event.

- Decide on how you will, as a co-parenting team, exercise parental power. Should parental responsibility be delegated (Mom takes care of sports, Dad takes care of music, stepmother takes care of homework, etc.)? How should the tasks of volunteering be divided? It is usually not a good idea for two parents and two stepparents to descend on a fourth-grade class to support one child. Who will be responsible for obtaining necessary supplies, such as art material, pencils, notebooks, and so on?

- Invisible co-parenting is the key to your child's school success. It is your job to avoid the teacher paradox. The entire co-parenting team should attend every conference, with Mom and Dad interacting with the teacher and stepparents listening. If a problem occurs, conduct an information call before talking to the school officials. Never involve your child's teacher in conflict. If you have significant differences as to how to solve a problem, obtain needed information, ask the teacher for an opinion, and discuss the issue at a special executive session. If needed, hire a mediator knowledgeable about school issues.

- Parents must decide on what to do with unanticipated events, such as emergencies, illness, bullies, honors, and so on.

- Your child's success in school depends in part on the capacity of the parenting team to move past conflict, which is destructive, to cooperation, which is synergy.

# CHAPTER 22

---

# Extended Family

Some of the more important relationships for any child are with his or her grandparents, aunts, uncles, cousins, and family friends. This extended family can offer children emotional support, a sense of pride and confidence, and an opportunity to be with an adult, other than a parent, who is willing to listen to their needs and love them for who they are.

To accommodate these important relationships, parents must be willing to permit unscheduled visits and, at times, extensions of visits. Parents will sometimes feel that "their time" is being infringed upon. It helps to think of it as the "child's time."

Sometimes, the family of one or both parents has entered the divorce conflict and is alienated from the other parent. When this happens, it is important for everyone to act maturely and focus only on the needs of the child, permitting the child to have contact with everyone.

Sometimes a parent is estranged from his or her own parents. If there are major problems, they should be aired before the final decree.

## Building an Extended Family

- Permit unplanned visits at the request of the other parent.
- Work to include your child in extended family activities, but understand the other parent's feelings and limit these visits so that you are not perceived as using relatives' visits as a way of gaining more parenting time.
- If a relative has a history of problems that may place your child in harm's way, work with the other parent to arrive at a plan that will assure your child's safety.
- If a family member is inappropriate, perhaps saying bad things about the absent parent, the related parent must intercede forcefully and directly, stopping such behavior. It is your responsibility to control your own family.
- Try to plan ahead for visits. Most often this is possible. However, when your child's favorite relative arrives with little notice, permit the visit so that your children will prosper.
- If one or both parents refuse to aid in extended family contact for no reason other than anger, the child suffers. Work with a mediator to solve the problem.
- Help your child gain a sense of the family and history by association with the extended family.

# CHAPTER 23

·····⊱⊰·····

# Extracurricular Activities

If a child is denied extracurricular activities, he or she is being short-changed in life, missing opportunities to have fun, to learn to cooperate, to handle aggressive feelings, and to learn how to win and lose. Often, when divorced parents are angry and not talking with each other, their child will not be able to participate in sports, camps, skill classes, music lessons, or other socially creative activities.

**Guidelines for Involving Your Child in Extracurricular Activities**
Parents must decide how many activities they want their child to join. Some parents overload their child. Other parents have too few activities. Decide on the number and type of activities within your budget, within your time schedules, and within your child's areas of interest and abilities.

Make sure your child wants to join an activity. If it is affordable and realistic, the child's choices should be honored. Some parents choose to rule out certain activities for safety or religious reasons.

Following are further guidelines for handling this issue:

- Before promising your child involvement in an activity, discuss it and come to an agreement with the other parent.
- Agree on which parent will coordinate each activity, based on interest and time.
- Agree on who will take your child to the activity and who will pay how much.
- Agree to make a mutual commitment and make sure your child can attend every event.
- Agree that both parents and stepparents can attend all activities and that the executive group will behave.
- If parents are unable to make such an agreement, seek mediation.
- When an activity overlaps both parents' time with the child, both parents must agree on all team activities, and both parents must be involved. Do not have the child in two different leagues or attending only half the games. Your child will never fit into the group and will always know you are fighting.

# CHAPTER 24

---

## Your Child's Friendships

Parents must carefully nurture and protect their child's social development. When a child lives in two homes and attends a school a long driving distance from either home, the issue of friendships becomes increasingly important. Many divorced children have three sets of friends: one set of friends at school and a set of friends at each home. No one knows exactly what impact this may have on a child's ability to form deep emotional commitments in the future. To err on the side of caution, divorced parents can work together to ensure that the children have constant friends and an opportunity to explore and develop new friendships.

As a child matures and becomes an adolescent, friendships must be closely monitored to avoid involvement in drugs, gangs, and premature sexual activity. You can help your child emancipate from the family in a responsible way. Your job is to permit your child to grow, mature, and become a self-sufficient adult. It may seem a tedious task—many parenting tasks are—but it is necessary to share information about your child's friendships.

## Building Friendships: A Checklist

- Can your child make friends reasonably easily, or is your child too shy or too aggressive?
- After forming a friendship, does your child maintain that friendship or quickly move on to other friends?
- Does your child gravitate to the "problem children" in class? This is indicative of low self-esteem.
- Does your child act too passively, unable to stand up to other children?
- Does your child intimidate or bully other children?
- Does your child attempt to buy friendships?
- Does your child belong to a circle of friends who are supportive, happy, and engaged in positive activities?
- Do you, as co-parents, agree on your assessment of your child's friends?
- Do you, as co-parents, support your child's need to seek out friends, to take the risk of being rejected, to tolerate teasing, to belong to a group, and to still be a thinking, independent individual?
- When your child loses a friend through death, accident, or moving away, can you, as co-parents, provide mutual support during the grieving process?
- Are you allowing your child to make appropriate social decisions to foster growth and maturity?
- Are you willing to provide the needed taxi service so that your child can be with school friends, friends from Dad's neighborhood, and friends from Mom's neighborhood?

# CHAPTER 25

---

# Hygiene

Parents will sometimes differ as to the routines of cleanliness, and these become issues for discussion. One parent may have the child bathe every evening. The other parent may have the child bathe "as needed," always returning the child dirty and disheveled to the first parent's care. One parent may insist the child brush his or her teeth after every meal and the other only once daily. A parent may send the child to school in the same clothes two days in a row, and the other parent may insist the child dress neatly in clean clothes daily. Mostly, these are irritating differences that can be easily modified. Sometimes one parent is trying to irritate the other parent. Such behavior needs to be addressed as a mutual problem, and failing a solution, the aggrieved parent must either accept the problem or seek mediation.

Occasionally a parent may be so negligent that the child's health is at risk, and the pediatrician or dentist must be involved. Such basic issues affecting health should be addressed with the assistance of a nurse, dentist, pediatrician, or other trained professional.

## Consider the Following Six Guidelines

- Children should bathe daily. If a parent has the children bathe more often or less often, parents should consult with the pediatrician for a guideline and then both follow the guideline.
- Send your children to school in clean and appropriate clothing. This does not require taking out a loan for the latest fad in sneakers.
- Ask your dentist for a routine dental care plan, with both parents following the plan.
- The children must be clean and appropriately dressed prior to the time of the exchange. If a parent returns a child dirty and sweaty, explaining they just got back from a bike ride that should create no problem. If the same problem is repeated the next two exchanges, and it is causing problems for you and your child, the parent returning the child needs to modify the schedule so that the exchanges occur in a less rushed fashion.
- Children can develop several disgusting habits: wearing the same pair of "favorite" pants every day for a month, spitting like a baseball player, nose-picking, and scratching (baseball players again). Parents need to discuss these behaviors and arrive at a consensus as to what to do. If Dad is proud that Junior spits every time he catches a ball, Mom is not likely to make Junior quit spitting.
- When lice come to visit—and they will—blame the lice, not the other parent, the school, or the other kids; just follow the delousing program. Parents should discuss the problem, agree on a course of action, and act. If needed, contact the school nurse. If only one parent tries to control lice, the efforts are doomed. This is a cooperative effort.

# CHAPTER 26

-----◆-----

# Friends and Family as Support Persons

This may come as a surprise to you, but there are people in this world who actually enjoy minding other people's business. These people often come disguised as friends, relatives, coworkers, and neighbors, as well as teachers and counselors. From whom you accept direction is your business.

## Making Advice Useful

- When anyone passes judgment on your co-parenting style, and they know only one parent and have heard only one side of the story, beware.
- Tell the well-meaning helper that the hardest part of divorce is trying to listen to the other parent without bias, and you would like for that person to present the other parent's position as clearly as possible. It is a quick and effective cure for the helper paradox.
- Grandparents can become very protective and are often willing to express their opinions freely. Appreciate their support and understand that they are biased and cannot give you objective guidance.

- Friends, coworkers, and even strangers sitting on the bar stool next to you may have just been through a divorce and will relive personal frustrating experiences through you. It is okay to listen, but don't let their problems become yours.

- New boyfriends or girlfriends, wanting to be helpful and protective, may offer all sorts of advice. Listen carefully, but remember the primary co-parenting responsibility is between the parents.

- When you come to believe that the other parent is being influenced by someone's advice, redouble your efforts to communicate about your children clearly and directly. It is usually not productive to tell the other parent that he or she is being taken as a fool.

- When the other parent complains that someone close to you is interfering with co-parenting, listen very closely. Then decide, for yourself—honestly—if your friend or relative is overstepping an important boundary.

- The very difficult task of co-parenting is to be shared by Mom and Dad. You must talk with each other, even though at times it may be painful to do so. One of the main things parents must learn after separating is that mind reading is not only impossible; it is dangerous to try. You can listen to other people's theories about the other parent. You can indulge in armchair psychiatry. But understand that is just a parlor game.

# CHAPTER 27

---

# Providing Medical and Dental Care

One of the more difficult problems for parents raising a child in two homes is providing good medical and dental care. Following are the biggest issues.

## Who Will Carry the Medical and Dental Insurance?

- How will the medical costs not covered by insurance be paid?
- What medical doctor and dentist will provide care to your child?
- Who will take your child for doctor and dentist visits?
- How will the other parent be informed of a medical emergency?

Arriving at a clear understanding is essential, not only for your peace of mind but also for your child's physical well-being. Without clear parent-to-parent communication about medical and dental needs, a child's welfare can be compromised.

Two parents described to me the importance of communication. Each had taken their child to a different pediatrician for an ear infection. Each was administering medication without checking with the other parent.

Their child fortunately was not hurt, but it made these caring parents aware of the need for communication about medical and dental care.

## Eleven Steps to Obtaining and Maintaining Medical and Dental Care for Your Child

- Select a primary pediatrician and dentist for your child, preferably close to the residential parent. If parents live far apart, select backup health care providers near the second parent for emergency care. Inform both sets of health care providers, in writing, of the name, telephone number, and address of the primary and backup care providers.

- If you wish to consult with another pediatrician, let the primary pediatrician and the other parent know before the appointment.

- Agree in writing as to who will pay for the insurance and the charges not covered by insurance.

- Review your health insurance plan yearly. Assess the plans realistically, and make your choices based on the needs of the child.

- Agree in writing as to who will take your child for routine medical and dental care. Some parents decide they both will accompany their child to such visits, to reduce the need for later intercommunication and as a way to support their child. Others decide that one parent will be responsible for routine care. Whatever is decided will work if both parents are aware of the plan and agree.

- Meet with health care providers as a co-parenting team to review your child's health and dental needs. Beware the medical paradox. If parents differ in their view of appropriate care, it is even more important they talk with the caregiver together.

- Understand the procedures for emergency care. Most parents will first take their child to the physician or hospital and then contact the other parent as soon as possible, taking into account the child's safety needs.

- If your child has chronic health problems, develop a plan with the help of your pediatrician to meet these problems.

- If you have differences of opinion regarding health care based on religious beliefs, talk with your religious counselors and with your pediatrician to determine how you will meet health concerns. If the differences are great—for example, one parent refusing transfusions and the other parent accepting transfusions—make sure you know how this is to be handled and communicate your decision to the health care provider before the need for a transfusion arises.

- If you have a difference of opinion about fluoride treatment, jointly discuss how you wish this handled with your dentist.

- Under no circumstances wait until the time of exchange to inform the other parent of a medical issue; for example, do not introduce your child's leg cast at the time of exchange.

# CHAPTER 28

---

# Values Training

Often parents do not deal directly with issues of morals, religion, and values systems. These may appear to be routine, relatively unimportant topics as you work out your co-parenting issues, but ultimately they are the issues that are most important.

What values do you each want to teach your children? Can you state them specifically, so that if problems develop, you can use these statements as a frame of reference? Suppose one parent finds it amusing that their eight-year-old is cheating at card games. The other parent may be upset about the cheating. By referring to your agreed-upon moral objectives, and hopefully agreeing that honesty is the best policy, you can decide how to work with your child as he learns the lessons of honesty and character, in part by playing board games with his family.

There are many resources on moral values that we can rely on: religious books, the *Desiderata*, the Golden Rule, the Scout Rules, and many others.

### Only Seven Steps to Achieving Shared Parenting Consistency
Sometimes parents disagree about having the children attend a specific church. Unless deep religious convictions are compromised, both parents

can exercise religious practices, taking the children to the church of choice on their parenting time.

- If one parent wants the other parent to take the children to the same church, a formal agreement should be reached.
- Many parents decided on the issues of religious training during marriage. Unless these decisions are renegotiated through mediation, they most likely should be honored after separation.
- If there is no agreement, or if a parent wants to change the agreement, it would be best to confer with a mediator and/or a religious counselor.
- When parents' religious values differ greatly, it is important to work out a plan that does not place the child in the middle of the conflict. If at all possible, let your child know that parents can differ in their religious beliefs, and these differences are recognized and protected.
- As with most teachings in life, children do what they see—not what they are told. The best teacher will be the example you set.

# CHAPTER 29

---◆-◇-◆---

# Parent–Child Telephone Calls

Telephone calls are often a major issue for divorced families. Telephones cross newly formed boundaries, sending a wired (or wireless) message from the heart of one home to the heart of the other. Children differ in how helpful a call is from the absent parent. Some children depend on such contact; others find that it simply generates homesickness.

## Thirteen Steps to Maximizing the Value of Parent/Child Communication

When separated by the parenting agreement, a parent and child have the right to talk by telephone each day for five minutes, except during vacations.

- The time must be appropriate, in keeping with the residential parent's schedule.
- The residential parent must not indicate by words, tone, or gestures that the call is not welcome, nor should that parent listen in on the call.
- If a child wants to "report" that the residential parent is mean or unfair, that is permissible. The parents should discuss the issue later.

- Telephone calls cannot be denied as a way to punish a child or a parent.
- If a parent calls and reaches an answering machine, say, "Hi, _____. How are you? I'll call you later. Please call me." Leave only positive messages that you want your child to hear.
- Keep the call positive, avoiding invoking homesickness by saying such things as "I miss you" or crying or relating some exciting event the child is missing.
- If the conversation lasts longer than five minutes, the residential parent must not interrupt the call unless there is a dire emergency. The issue should be discussed between the parents at a later time.
- If you promise to call, do so, unless you have a good excuse and the surgery bills to back up your statements.
- Never promise your child a special treat upon returning to your home.
- Even though the absent parent can call daily, don't. Make the schedule variable. Let the child initiate the call. The residential parent can encourage the child to call.
- Discuss as co-parents the effects of telephone calls. Some children like and are comforted by calls. Others are bored. Still other children become upset. Make sure you are meeting the needs of your child by making the call, not just your needs.
- The rules for cell phone and e-mail use have not been clearly established, so consider yourself part of a new cultural phenomenon, helping to develop new rules. For example, should a one-year-old child have his or her own cell phone and, if so, a private number?

# CHAPTER 30

------ ◆◆◆ ------

# Boundaries

Boundaries must be carefully observed when raising a child who lives with two families and in two homes. If parents observe the following thirteen guidelines, the anger quotient will be greatly reduced:

1.  Have your child sleep in his or her own bed. There are many problems with the practice of sleeping with your child. For example, you can be accused of child molestation. In our society, children must learn to be individuals at a very early age. Sleeping alone is one way this is learned. If one parent permits the child to sleep with him or her, the other parent will have great difficulty enforcing the separate bed rule. Children must learn to face and deal with their fears. You can help your child do this by making bedtime pleasant and the child's bed a place of safety and security. Rather than let your child go to bed with you, read to your child until he or she falls sleep. Work together as co-parents to help your child learn how to sleep alone.
2.  Be a parent, not a "buddy." The roles of parent and child must be kept separate and clear. If you are lonely for a companion, go find a friend your own age.

3. Talk to your child about appropriate issues, not the divorce or the shortcomings of the other parent.

4. Children do not understand the concept of money any more than adults do. Talk to your child about things both of you can understand. But never about money or divorce issues.

5. If punishment of your child is necessary, do it yourself. Do not permit your friends, live-in partner, or other relatives to punish your child. Never let anyone else spank your child, not even Grandma. Use a brief time-out to correct behavior—not as a threat or as a punishment, but as a way to interrupt unwanted behavior so that you can direct your child to better behavior.

6. Do not quiz your child about events in the other parent's house— who is there, where they go, what they do, or what is said. Listen to your child, and if you hear about problematic behavior, talk directly to the other parent.

7. Refer to the other parent as Mom or Dad, not by cruel nicknames.

8. Accept your parenting plan as it is now, and do what you can to make it work.

9. Expend your energy becoming effective parents rather than fighting. There is no such thing as a perfect parenting plan. All plans are compromises.

10. When you, as co-parents, are no longer in conflict, are responding to each other in a business-like manner, and are permitting your child to have easy access to each parent, your child will have the potential for a successful post-separation adjustment.

11. Accept that you now have new boundaries and must respect the other parent's privacy.

12. Accept that each parent has a different view of the marriage and divorce, and neither can change the other's point of view. Attempting to convince the other parent of your point of view regarding the separation and divorce is an attempt to gain that parent's approval. By getting divorced, you have forever neutralized the mechanism for getting the other parent's approval.

13. Accept the past and work for your child's future.

# CHAPTER 31

———◆◇◆———

# Safety

Parents have the right and responsibility to know their child is safe. We all know that safety is a relative word. As children learn, grow, and explore the world, they may be injured. But do follow these guidelines:

- Make sure your child is safe. Some basic rules include no playing in the parking lot of the new apartment, no swimming alone, no staying alone at the park, no riding a bike on a busy street, no unprotected weapons in the house, no poisons under the sink, and no razor blades left on the counter.
- Let the other parent know you are attending to safety issues. One of the major losses in divorce is the ability to protect your child at all times. You must leave the child's safety in the hands of the person you decided you no longer want to be with. I have seen parents try to punish each other by not reassuring each other of the child's safety. This is cruel and not a part of effective co-parenting.
- Sometimes parents differ as to what is safe and what is not. Some activities, we all know are unsafe. We all know that as a child

grows, there will be risks that foster the development of bravery and autonomy. But what if one parent objects to the other letting their three-year-old play in the backyard alone for thirty minutes? The best resolution is to ask someone who knows about such issues—a teacher, a pediatrician, a child psychologist, and other parents of three-year-old children. Within reason it is better to err in the direction of safety. Sometimes a parent is a fearful person, and if things were his or her way, the child would live in a plastic bubble in washed and purified air. Then it is time to consult a therapist knowledgeable about safety issues to determine whether the fearful parent is transferring fears to the child.

- We are living in an era in which we hear and read daily of abducted and murdered children. Most of the children who talk with me tell me about their night fears—that the current monster seen on the evening news has abducted, raped, and mutilated a small child. About all we can do is work hard to make people better, eradicate poverty, reinvent hope, lock up bad people, and teach our children how to be safe and alert to the dangers of the world.

- Sometimes children are injured. It is easy for an angry divorced parent to blame the other parent. It would be exceedingly rare for a parent to want a child hurt. But accidents do happen. When they do, it is important for co-parents to be supportive and not blaming.

# CHAPTER 32

---

# Safe Sexual Development

There are two issues to cover in the area of sexuality: protecting from harm and encouraging appropriate development.

## Safety from Sexual Predators

Monitor your child's behavior to observe any change in sexual interest or activity. If there is a change, this must be discussed with the other parent. It is possible someone is molesting your child outside of your home—a classmate, an adult in a position of authority or trust, or a stranger.

It is difficult to discuss the issue of molestation with the other parent because it is a sensitive issue. During the late 1980s and early '90s, there was a trend in which one of the parents would accuse the other parent of molesting the child as a way to gain full custody. Some people believe that there has been an increase in molestations by a parent after divorce because a parent is vulnerable and needs support or is angry and acting out against the other parent.

Even though it is difficult, it is necessary to discuss with the other parent any change you observe in your child's sexual adjustment. The more obvious symptoms are increased sexual play, unusual curiosity about adult body parts, nightmares, sudden onset of bedwetting, and open masturbation. Keep in mind that some sex play is normal. Also keep in mind that other life events can cause each of these symptoms. Don't jump to conclusions. Discuss your concerns with the other parent, your pediatrician, or a therapist.

## A Safe Sexual Development

It is your responsibility as parents to help your child grow up to be a happy, well-adjusted adult with clear gender identification.

One school of thought maintains that homosexuality is genetically based. Another school of thought maintains that homosexuality is learned. If gender identification issues are noted, parents must be alert to their child's needs, discuss the issue, and decide on a course of action that is in the child's best interest.

# CHAPTER 33

---

# Transportation

The issue of transportation can be a difficult and persistent problem. If parents are willing to work out a plan, it can become a nonproblem.

- The receiving parent provides transportation.
- Parents decide at the outset who will take the children to the pediatrician, dentist, therapist, and so on.
- Parents decide at the outset who will provide school transportation.
- The decisions regarding transportation can easily be resolved if they are based on (a) which parent is available and (b) an even distribution of travel time.
- Regardless of your concerns about travel, it is less of a problem for each parent than it is for your child.
- Use travel time as an opportunity to talk, play games, and enjoy being with your child.
- Your child did not want the divorce and should not suffer because of it. If a child needs transportation to a show, to an activity, to

visit a friend, or for anything else, either parent should be available to provide taxi service without expecting payback.

- If transportation clearly gets out of balance, and one parent is saddled with the taxi-chore most of the time, meet together and come up with a better decision. If you can't, talk with a mediator.

- Determining a transportation schedule is the responsibility of parents and is not an issue to be discussed with your child beyond seeking age-appropriate input.

# CHAPTER 34

## Peaceful Exchanges

Moving a child from one home to the next is a focal point of the old and new system. It is the one time when the old family is reunited. The losses are felt more keenly because it also represents a parent losing a child and a child losing a parent—if only for overnight. Many parents report difficulty in making the exchanges.

### A Formula for Peaceful Exchanges

1. If your child is visibly upset at the time of the exchange, something is wrong. Determine what it might be. If it is obvious, fix it. Do not assume that either parent is at fault. If you don't know what is causing the upset, seek professional help.
2. If a child is visibly upset but calms down a few minutes after being alone with the receiving parent, it still means that something is wrong. Determine what that is and correct it.
3. At the time of exchange, use the following procedure:
   a. The parent bringing the child (parent A) goes with the child to the door of the other parent (parent B).

b. Parent B invites parent A into the house. Parent A does not assume an invitation and must wait until the invitation is made. This is a new and important boundary issue.

c. Parents make small talk, discussing the weather and other neutral topics.

d. Parents do not discuss any co-parenting issue. The only task at the time of exchange is helping your child move from one home to the other.

e. Do not, out of discomfort, focus on the child. Many parents do this, causing the child to be uncomfortable.

f. Permit the child to observe both parents and slowly become accustomed to the change.

g. Children make an internal switch from one parent to the other. As parents talk, the child will usually join in and begin talking to parent B (the receiving parent).

h. When parents observe the child moving to parent B (talking, holding hands, etc.), parent A says good-bye and leaves.

4. The internal adjustment of the child, if not interfered with by parental conflict, usually takes five to ten minutes. If the child does not make the internal adjustment of moving toward the receiving parent, something is wrong. Usually the exchange was too rushed, or the parents were in conflict. A child is very sensitive to parental feelings, and even if parents are hiding conflict, a child will know that the parents are angry with one another.

5. Parent B must avoid intimidating the child with too many questions or too effusive a greeting, permitting the child to make the transition easily.

6. Parent A must avoid using "hot" words that will evoke homesickness, envy, or concerns in the child. Do not make such remarks as the following: "You *have* to visit with Mom." "I will miss you." "We are taking your stepbrother to Disneyland, so we won't be back until Tuesday." "When you get home, we have a big surprise for you." "I'm going to cry." "I feel like I will die when I have to leave

you here." These are examples. You can come up with many more hot phrases that need to be avoided.

7. At the following weekly telephone call, discuss how your child is reacting to the exchange. The purpose is not to attempt to change the parenting schedule, but to make the exchange as smooth and peaceful as possible.

# CHAPTER 35

---

## Vacations and Holidays

A n area of major disagreement for co-parents is unscheduled events. The day before major holidays is marred for many divorced parents, arguing over who will have parenting time with their child.

### Four Simple Steps to Avoiding Holiday Conflicts

1. Parents must agree on all vacations and holiday times in advance and then confirm these times during the semiyearly meetings.

2. Co-parenting is inherently more difficult than one-home parenting and takes more time to do appropriately. Parents feel frustrated because decision making and planning for co-parenting is such a lengthy process. Many parents assume they know the custody schedule and launch into a discussion of an upcoming holiday without reviewing their written agreement. Working together as co-parents will promote no conflicted exchanges at holiday and vacation times.

3. In addition to verbally confirming holiday schedules, it is helpful to put them in writing and send a copy to the other parent.

4. It is helpful to have default plans for holidays and vacations. If a parent fails to make clear arrangements, or if the other parent fails to confirm, rely on the default holiday schedule in your parenting plans.

# CHAPTER 36

---

# Problem Solving and Managing Crises

Follow these rules, and you can improve your decision-making ability. When you were together and beginning to experience problems leading to divorce, your ability to make joint decisions became impaired. The usual reasons include the use of power and the absence of mutual regard. Now you need to learn to make decisions much as a social club, in which no one is all-powerful, and the members have distant, formal respect for each other but a common goal. In this type of decision making, the goal is the well-being of your child.

## Eight Simple Steps to Making Co-parent Decisions

1. State the problem clearly. Often parents will forget to state the problem, and the resulting discussion is frustrating for everyone. Even though this seems to be a simple task, it is the hardest one when it comes to making a decision.

2. Each parent should offer at least two solutions. When attempting to solve a problem, we can fall in love with our first solution. To be creative and to actually solve problems, state at least two

solutions. Sometimes parents will agree on a solution at this point.

3. If agreement is not reached, determine what information is needed to make an informed decision. For example, if you are working toward having your child on a baseball team, you need to know who will be the coach, what is expected of your child and each of you, when and where practice and games are held, and how you will make sure your child belongs, has transportation, and is supported, emotionally and financially. You have probably noticed that gaining information follows the same rules as a newspaper article: Who, what, when, where, and how?

4. After gaining information, discuss the issue again, focusing on the needs of your child.

5. If you arrive at a decision, good.

6. If you don't arrive at a decision, you may need the help of a mediator trained in decision-making skills. The mediator will assist you in making the decision, help you understand the decision-making process, and point out the problems that make decision making difficult for you.

7. When a decision is made, determine when it will be put into action.

8. Set a time in the future when you will check to make sure your decision is working. The best thing about making a decision is that if it doesn't work, all you have to do is make another decision. Practice makes perfect.

## Managing Crises

Parents have told me that after years of conducting the business of raising a child in two homes, they'd thought they were past the anger and hurt of their marriage. Then one day, while discussing an issue regarding their child, their anger reemerged as if they had separated the day before. In such cases, both parents are surprised that so much anger was lying dormant for so long. They often feel defeated, as if they will never move past the intimate anger stage. Even when experiencing anger from the past, parents should keep in mind that they still have good co-parenting skills; they have not regressed. They do not need to start over but can examine what happened, correct it, and move on. There are several major reasons that old anger reemerges as if it were new. They are discussed in the following sections.

## Child Enters a New Developmental Stage

When the children enter a new developmental stage, the previous parenting plan is no longer effective, and parents must renegotiate.

Fran and Nathan separated when Nancy was three years old. Nancy was almost toilet trained at the time, but regressed, once again wetting the bed. She was also having bad dreams.

Fran and Nathan were experiencing a living nightmare. They fought each other every inch of the way. They each had hired an attorney that complemented their desire to "get" the other parent. The divorce took only a year, but by the end of the year, both parents were broke, living with their parents, and emotionally drained and financially exhausted by the ordeal.

Over the next year each was able to rebuild a life. They had been able to keep their jobs, and each had purchased a condo. Neither had jumped into a new relationship, still reeling from the acrimony of divorce. After the divorce was final, they were able to talk and agreed to put their anger behind them, focusing only on the needs of Nancy. Fran was the residential parent. Nathan and Nancy were together every Wednesday after school for four hours and every other weekend. Fran and Nathan were very focused on their child's needs. They were quite pleased with how well they had learned to be good co-parents.

When Nancy was almost five, Fran and Nathan were talking about Nancy beginning school in a few months. Nathan said, "I took her to Kingston Elementary so she could get used to her new school."

Fran was taken aback. "You did what? You know better than that! You always were controlling! How dare you pick a school and not talk to me about it?"

Nathan expressed surprise and explained that Kingston was just around the corner from his house and only a mile from Fran's house. He had assumed that was where Nancy would attend school.

"Assumed!" shouted Fran. "I thought we were past you trying to control everything and everyone around you. I am going to see my attorney and get this straightened out."

The parents were only vaguely aware that Nancy was present and heard their argument. That evening she was very quiet. As she was getting ready for bed, she told her mother she didn't want to go to school. Mom shrugged off her comments, saying, "Of course you do. We have talked about how much fun you will have. Now go to sleep and have good dreams."

Nancy went to sleep and woke up from a nightmare about two monsters fighting in her room. Fran realized that she and Nathan had made a big mistake. She told Nancy, "Dad and I will talk about school today. We want you to be happy in school, and we are not sure which school would be best."

Morosely, Nancy said, "All my friends are going to Kingston."

The sudden surge of anger that overwhelmed Fran and Nathan is not unusual, and it doesn't mean they had failed as co-parents. They were simply unprepared when Nancy was entering a new developmental age. Many new decisions would have to be made. They had been "coasting" for almost a year, getting into a routine and sharing information, and had forgotten how difficult it is to make decisions as co-parents.

## Parents Can Run into Hidden Boundaries

Boundary issues that neither parent knew about can be violated. When these hidden boundary issues emerge, tempers can flair.

For example, if Dad's parents rarely visit and haven't been in town since the separation, they could inadvertently assume it would be okay to see their grandson at school and drive by to surprise him. However, Mom is very careful about her son's safety. She had given him strict orders to come home from school immediately. That day, she stopped by to pick him up and saw his grandparents talking to him. To Mom, this was an infringement of a boundary.

## A Change in the Balance of Power

The balance of power can change when either parent forms a new relationship. Often, well-functioning co-parents will enter into a difficult phase.

For example, if Mom hears from her daughter all about Dad's new girlfriend, she may become jealous, feeling her mother role is being jeopardized, and her daughter will like the stepmom more than her. Old feelings regarding her ex can emerge. Even though she would not want him back, she resents that this avenue is now being closed off.

Or Dad can hear that Mom has a boyfriend who is taking Dad's son fishing and coaching his baseball team. Many feelings can emerge, with Dad feeling threatened.

Worse, a new partner can support a parent who has been complaining about the parenting plan. With the new partner's support, the parent may want to go back to court.

Or even worse yet, a new partner can try to subvert the parenting plan. One way is to subtly try to reduce the amount of time the "little tyrant" is in the house. The other extreme is for the new partner to demand that the other parent never come over again.

## A Parent Wants to Move Away

Anger can erupt when one parent wants to move across town, to another city, or to another state, requiring that parents relive their custody dispute once again.

## Co-parents Become Complacent

Parents can become complacent co-parents when everything is going reasonably well. They quit making their weekly telephone call and stop meeting for long-term planning. Many issues remain unresolved. But after a while, the amount of work and time that co-parenting takes makes one or both parents edgy and one parent reacts irritably toward the other.

## When Parents Have an Honest Difference about What Is Best for the Child

Sometimes parents will disagree about what is best for their child and discover they lack the capacity to make an effective decision. For example, the other parent, "for no good reason," disagrees with what you want to do for your child. Your child may need special attention at school, and you have received information that a private school nearby can supply exactly what your child needs. However, the other parent simply says, "No, I can't afford it, and I don't like the idea of private schools anyway. So let's just follow our parenting plan."

It is helpful to understand the sources of old anger. There are many forces working to activate and renew your old anger. Be aware of them. Be in charge of them. You control these forces. Don't let the forces control you. Here are some things you can do to continue on the path of shared parenting.

## Twenty Things to Do When Disaster Strikes

1. First, realize that what you are experiencing is normal and does not mean you have failed as a co-parent.
2. Accept your parenting plan as it is now and do what you can to make it work.
3. Accept the past and work for your child's future.
4. Expend your energy becoming effective co-parents rather than fighting. Ask yourself if arguing with the other parent is serving your child or your anger.
5. Accept that you now have new boundaries and respect the other parent's privacy.
6. Accept that each parent has a different view of the marriage and divorce, and neither can change the other's point of view. Attempting to convince the other parent of your point of view regarding the separation and divorce is an attempt to gain that parent's approval. By getting divorced, you have forever given up the mechanism of getting the other parent's unconditional approval.
7. Understand that everyone at times is a "malicious" parent and that your petty, revengeful feelings are transient.
8. Write a letter of apology to the other parent. You need not send it.
9. Expand and enrich your own life, understanding that the crisis of divorce will pass, and you can experience positive personal growth and change.

10. Remember that your child needs you and will profit from your personal enjoyment of life.

11. Remember that the goal is to move from intimate anger to the business of shared parenting.

12. Each parent must individually resolve the remaining aspects of the intimate relationship. It cannot be done together.

13. Each parent can preserve the good memories of the relationship as proof that your child did have good times when the family was together and that each parent has the capacity to be a good partner.

14. To the extent you can, without dwelling on mistakes, profit from your mistakes, make changes, and move on.

15. Each parent must face and reconcile the many losses that occur when a major relationship is dissolved. It does no good to blame the other parent. Accept that each parent has made mistakes, and you must address the mistakes you made and make corrections. Otherwise, you give all your strength to the other parent.

16. Remember that revenge only hurts the children.

17. Before making a retaliatory comment or action against the other parent, ask yourself whether the comment will improve the life of your child. If it won't—and it usually won't—then don't make the comment.

18. You probably tried and failed to change the other parent while you were together. The likelihood is even less that you can change the other parent now. What you see and hear is what you get. Make sure you see and hear accurately, unbiased by the prism of your discontent.

19. Every marriage has a thousand boundaries, all of which change after separation. Co-parents will experience strong feelings of anger when one or both parents assume a marriage boundary is still operative.

20. Here are a few alarm statements to let you know when you are violating new boundaries:
    - I built the door. I installed the lock. I have a key. I will come into that house anytime I please!

- What are you going to do the weekend I have our daughter?
- How much of my money are you squirreling away?
- You never changed a diaper. What makes you think you are going to learn now?
- You wanted the divorce; now our child is in need of therapy! I hope you're happy!
- You wanna step outside this bar and say that?

# PART 5

————— ❖ —————

# Epilogue and Appendices

Part 5 includes the book's epilogue; several forms, checklists, scripts, and so on that you can use to help co-parent communication; and a final request from the author for feedback.

# Epilogue

When parents separate, it is usually mutual, agreed upon by both. One may say the magic words, "I want a divorce," more often. One may hire an attorney first. One may file first. That one may be the most courageous, able to put into words what is in the heart of each.

But regardless, it is time to change, to begin anew and face the unknown. Parents often view this as a time of desperation, having "tried everything" and then resolved that the only way to peace and sanity was to separate and build a new life. What usually begins out of desperation can become a voyage of enlightenment. However, the trip may be difficult. You know the perils of getting from intimate anger to the business of co-parenting.

For most divorcing parents, there is that defining moment when the emotions shift and the possibility of reconciliation becomes remote. It is at this moment that the parents can say what is wanted and what is not wanted. They don't want the oppressive quality of the relationship they are leaving. They do want freedom, lightness, someone to validate them, and relief from the worry and guilt of a distressed marriage.

What does the future hold for you? Most often it is remarriage. Quite often it is stepchildren. Sometimes it is new children with a new partner. Most relationships start simply. And most, if they endure, include elements of being constricting and confining. The alternative is being alone, or at least perceiving oneself to be alone. Yet being in a relationship is probably built into our genetic structure as surely as baby blue or soft brown eyes. At the beginning of this book, I encouraged you to make your present marriage work. Upon taking one more look at your marriage, perhaps some of you will stay together. Others of you will divorce. And if you have performed due diligence, it is a no-fault divorce. You didn't just jump into divorce impulsively. You thought about the pros and cons. You considered alternatives, and then decided it would be better for you and the other parent to raise your child in two homes.

From that point on, this book has been about how you can make the transition easier. I am convinced that most divorcing parents fight because they don't know how not to fight. This book has been about learning how not to fight and how to instead solve problems and develop a positive new life. Divorce is a difficult process under any circumstances. I hope my attempts at humor were taken in the spirit intended; I hope that you will not take yourself too seriously and understand that it takes a while to recover from the process.

Your child doesn't have the power and control that you do. If you feel powerless at times, imagine how your child feels. Research on the effects of family transition tells us that a child of divorce does have more problems than a child in a one-home family.

What is really important is that the same research tells us that if you as co-parents can leave your conflict behind and move on with your own lives, your children can make a positive adjustment. It has been my privilege to work with parents and hear that their children have become less depressed and less argumentative. The only things that changed were the parents' lower degree of conflict, improved parent-to-parent communication, and a mature desire to permit their child easy access to both parents. You can make a difference. Your vow that your children wouldn't be hurt by the divorce can be honored.

# APPENDIX A

---

# Assessing Your Skills as a Co-parent

1. ACCEPTING PERSONAL RESPONSIBILITY

We no longer place all the blame on the other parent and have now reached the point of understanding that each is now responsible for our own shared-parenting skills.

Cannot do at all    1    2    3    4    5    Perform easily   _____

We no longer seek the approval of the other parent, realizing that the need for such approval is a carryover from our previous relationship. We now understand that we each must act independently, yet still work together in the best interest of our child.

Cannot do at all    1    2    3    4    5    Perform easily   _____

2. MAINTAINING BOUNDARIES BETWEEN OUR
   HOMES

We have reached the point of being able to act independently, keeping each other informed of our thoughts, plans, and actions regarding our child, but not forced to give details of our everyday life.

Cannot do at all    1    2    3    4    5    Perform easily    _____

We understand and agree that as co-parents we must communicate between ourselves and not pass messages through our child.

Cannot do at all    1    2    3    4    5    Perform easily    _____

We understand that arguing has nothing to do with problem solving. We have moved past arguing, realizing that to argue is self-indulgent and harmful to our child.

Cannot do at all    1    2    3    4    5    Perform easily    _____

We understand that we must learn new decision-making skills. If we hold different opinions about how best to meet the needs of our child, we will first discuss the issue between ourselves. If we are unable to come to a decision, we will meet with a mediator so that a decision can be appropriately reached.

Cannot do at all    1    2    3    4    5    Perform easily    _____

3. EFFECTIVE PARENT-TO-PARENT
   COMMUNICATION

We have developed a no-fault, nondefensive way of communicating urgent messages regarding our child's daily needs.

Cannot do at all    1    2    3    4    5    Perform easily    _____

We have developed a system of regular parent-to-parent phone calls to share ongoing information regarding our child in a business-like manner.

    Cannot do at all    1   2   3   4   5    Perform easily   _____

We have developed a system of communication about the long-range needs of our child.

    Cannot do at all    1   2   3   4   5    Perform easily   _____

## 4. SUPPORTING THE OTHER PARENT'S POSITIVE TRAITS

We want our child to have the best of both parents, and we support each other's positive traits in the eyes of our child.

    Cannot do at all    1   2   3   4   5    Perform easily   _____

## 5. DEVELOPING A POWERFUL CO-PARENTING TEAM

We understand that the co-parenting team consists of parents and stepparents. We are developing ways to use the skills and abilities of all team members to enhance the life of our child.

    Cannot do at all    1   2   3   4   5    Perform easily   _____

We understand that if the co-parenting team is in conflict, our child will suffer, and when the co-parenting team is working cooperatively, the combined skills can enhance our child's life.

    Cannot do at all    1   2   3   4   5    Perform easily   _____

## 6.  PROVIDING EASY ACCESS TO EACH PARENT

We have the ability to allow our child easy access to each parent.

Cannot do at all    1    2    3    4    5    Perform easily    _____

## 7.  DEVELOPING AN EFFECTIVE, PUBLIC CO-PARENTING TEAM

We understand that co-parenting should be invisible to teachers, scout leaders, and other persons who have frequent contact with our child, that we should not air our problems in public.

Cannot do at all    1    2    3    4    5    Perform easily    _____

We have learned to play zone defense when we meet in public, permitting easy, conflict-free interchange between parent and child.

Cannot do at all    1    2    3    4    5    Perform easily    _____

We have learned that our child is sensitive to our conflicts and is easily embarrassed if we argue in public.

Cannot do at all    1    2    3    4    5    Perform easily    _____

## 8.  MONITORING OUR CHILD'S WELFARE

We have learned that we must, in a no-fault manner, communicate regarding our child's welfare, sharing both positive and negative information.

Cannot do at all    1    2    3    4    5    Perform easily    _____

## 9. AVOIDING POWER STRUGGLES

We know it takes two to have a power struggle. When we engage in a win/lose argument our child always loses.

Cannot do at all     1   2   3   4   5     Perform easily     _____

We understand that when a marital relationship ends, only the impasse issues remain. As effective co-parents, when we are faced with an impasse issue, we move on without becoming embroiled in bitter conflict.

Cannot do at all     1   2   3   4   5     Perform easily     _____

## 10. MOVING ON, EMOTIONALLY AND PHYSICALLY

We have moved from the crisis of divorce to the understanding that although we have chosen not to live together, we will share the task of raising our child in a responsible, mature manner.

Cannot do at all     1   2   3   4   5     Perform easily     _____

We understand that we have physically separated and that the process of emotional separation will take time. We respect each other's independence and understand that our only connection is our child, whom we agree to raise to be a happy, self-assured, responsible adult.

Cannot do at all     1   2   3   4   5     Perform easily     _____

# APPENDIX B

———————————

# Co-parent Checklist

*Make as many copies as you want*

5 = No problem, doing well; 1 = Major problem, proceed with caution

1.  Alternative care                    1   2   3   4   5

   _____

   _____


2.  Behavior and discipline          1   2   3   4   5

   _____

   _____


3.  Counseling and therapy          1   2   3   4   5

   _____

   _____

4.   Clothing                              1   2   3   4   5

_____

_____


5.   Parent–parent–teacher cooperation     1   2   3   4   5

_____

_____


6.   Giving your child an extended family   1   2   3   4   5

_____

_____


7.   Extracurricular activities             1   2   3   4   5

_____

_____


8.   Guiding your child's friendships       1   2   3   4   5

_____

_____


9.   Hygiene                                1   2   3   4   5

_____

_____


10.  Teaching friends and relatives to behave   1   2   3   4   5

_____

_____


11.  Providing medical and dental care      1   2   3   4   5

_____

_____

12. Values training                                1  2  3  4  5

_____

_____

13. Parent–child telephone calls                   1  2  3  4  5

_____

_____

14. Maintaining parent–child boundaries            1  2  3  4  5

_____

_____

15. Safety                                         1  2  3  4  5

_____

_____

16. Safe sexual development                        1  2  3  4  5

_____

_____

17. Transportation                                 1  2  3  4  5

_____

_____

18. Peaceful exchanges                             1  2  3  4  5

_____

_____

19. Vacation and holiday planning                  1  2  3  4  5

_____

_____

20.   Problem solving and crisis control          1    2    3    4    5

_____

_____

# APPENDIX C

---

# Behavior Checklist

*Make as many copies as you wish*

Rate your child's behavior: 1 = major problem; 5 = doing well.

Mother should circle her score; father should draw a square around his score.

Combine parents' scores for each item and then combine totals for each area of behavior.

| Behavior | Parents' Ratings | Mother and Father Total |
|---|---|---|
| Argumentative | 1  2  3  4  5 | _____ |
| Bullies others | 1  2  3  4  5 | _____ |
| Disobedient | 1  2  3  4  5 | _____ |
| Stubborn | 1  2  3  4  5 | _____ |
| **EXTERNALIZING BEHAVIOR** | | _____ |

| | | | | | | | |
|---|---|---|---|---|---|---|---|
| Teases others | 1 | 2 | 3 | 4 | 5 | | _____ |
| Withdrawn | 1 | 2 | 3 | 4 | 5 | | _____ |
| Lacks energy | 1 | 2 | 3 | 4 | 5 | | _____ |
| Stares blankly | 1 | 2 | 3 | 4 | 5 | | _____ |
| Secretive | 1 | 2 | 3 | 4 | 5 | | _____ |
| Refuses to talk | 1 | 2 | 3 | 4 | 5 | | _____ |

WITHDRAWING BEHAVIOR _____

| | | | | | | | |
|---|---|---|---|---|---|---|---|
| Steals | 1 | 2 | 3 | 4 | 5 | | _____ |
| Cheats | 1 | 2 | 3 | 4 | 5 | | _____ |
| Runs away | 1 | 2 | 3 | 4 | 5 | | _____ |
| Lies | 1 | 2 | 3 | 4 | 5 | | _____ |
| Bad friends | 1 | 2 | 3 | 4 | 5 | | _____ |

ANTISOCIAL BEHAVIOR _____

| | | | | | | | |
|---|---|---|---|---|---|---|---|
| Aches and pains | 1 | 2 | 3 | 4 | 5 | | _____ |
| Headaches | 1 | 2 | 3 | 4 | 5 | | _____ |
| Sickly | 1 | 2 | 3 | 4 | 5 | | _____ |
| Stomach aches | 1 | 2 | 3 | 4 | 5 | | _____ |
| Nausea | 1 | 2 | 3 | 4 | 5 | | _____ |

ACHES AND PAINS _____

| | | | | | | | |
|---|---|---|---|---|---|---|---|
| Anxious | 1 | 2 | 3 | 4 | 5 | | _____ |
| Fearful | 1 | 2 | 3 | 4 | 5 | | _____ |
| Low self-esteem | 1 | 2 | 3 | 4 | 5 | | _____ |
| Sad, depressed | 1 | 2 | 3 | 4 | 5 | | _____ |
| Worries a lot | 1 | 2 | 3 | 4 | 5 | | _____ |

DEPRESSION _____

| | | | | | | |
|---|---|---|---|---|---|---|
| Stays awake | 1 | 2 | 3 | 4 | 5 | _____ |
| Bad dreams | 1 | 2 | 3 | 4 | 5 | _____ |
| Wets bed | 1 | 2 | 3 | 4 | 5 | _____ |
| Sleeps too much | 1 | 2 | 3 | 4 | 5 | _____ |
| Wakes too early | 1 | 2 | 3 | 4 | 5 | _____ |
| SLEEP ADJUSTMENT | | | | | | _____ |

| | | | | | | |
|---|---|---|---|---|---|---|
| Picky eater | 1 | 2 | 3 | 4 | 5 | _____ |
| Overeater | 1 | 2 | 3 | 4 | 5 | _____ |
| Junk food preference | 1 | 2 | 3 | 4 | 5 | _____ |
| Resists new foods | 1 | 2 | 3 | 4 | 5 | _____ |
| Eats too little | 1 | 2 | 3 | 4 | 5 | _____ |
| EATING ADJUSTMENT | | | | | | _____ |

| | | | | | | |
|---|---|---|---|---|---|---|
| Teacher conflict | 1 | 2 | 3 | 4 | 5 | _____ |
| Peer conflict | 1 | 2 | 3 | 4 | 5 | _____ |
| Homework conflict | 1 | 2 | 3 | 4 | 5 | _____ |
| Grades below ability | 1 | 2 | 3 | 4 | 5 | _____ |
| Not motivated | 1 | 2 | 3 | 4 | 5 | _____ |
| SCHOOL ADJUSTMENT | | | | | | _____ |

| | | | | | | |
|---|---|---|---|---|---|---|
| Leaves things behind | 1 | 2 | 3 | 4 | 5 | _____ |
| Complains about plans | 1 | 2 | 3 | 4 | 5 | _____ |
| Angry at parent(s) | 1 | 2 | 3 | 4 | 5 | _____ |
| Resists exchange | 1 | 2 | 3 | 4 | 5 | _____ |
| Long adjustment time | 1 | 2 | 3 | 4 | 5 | _____ |
| TRANSITION PROBLEMS | | | | | | _____ |

| | | | | | | | |
|---|---|---|---|---|---|---|---|
| Loyalty conflicts | 1 | 2 | 3 | 4 | 5 | | _____ |
| Guilt about divorce | 1 | 2 | 3 | 4 | 5 | | _____ |
| Distant from parent(s) | 1 | 2 | 3 | 4 | 5 | | _____ |
| Angry at both parents | 1 | 2 | 3 | 4 | 5 | | _____ |
| Slow adjustment | 1 | 2 | 3 | 4 | 5 | | _____ |

DIVORCE ADJUSTMENT                                              _____

_____

_____

_____

_____

_____

_____

_____

# APPENDIX D

## Agenda for Semiyearly Meeting

**February**

*Make as many copies as you wish*

Meeting location _____ Date _____

Lincoln's/MLK's Birthday

_____

_____

Presidents Day

_____

_____

Passover

_____

_____

Easter

_____

_____

Spring Break

_____

_____

Mother's Day

_____

_____

Memorial Day

_____

_____

Father's Day

_____

_____

Independence Day

_____

_____

Formal vacations

_____

_____

Birthdays

_____

_____

Other

_____

_____

Extracurricular

_____

_____

School activities

_____

_____

Assessment of child and need for action (education, social, rules, happiness, and morals)

_____

_____

Decisions made during this semiyearly meeting

_____

_____

_____

_____

_____

_____

_____

_____

# APPENDIX E

# Agenda for Semiyearly Meeting

**August**

*Make as many copies as you wish*

Location ________________________________ Date _______________

Labor Day

_______________________________________________________________

_______________________________________________________________

Columbus Day

_______________________________________________________________

_______________________________________________________________

Halloween

_____

_____

Veterans Day

_____

_____

Thanksgiving

_____

_____

Chanukah

_____

_____

Christmas Vacation

_____

_____

Christmas Eve/Day

_____

_____

New Year's

_____

_____

Formal vacations

_____

_____

Birthdays

_____

_____

_____

_____

Other

_____

_____

Extracurricular

_____

_____

_____

_____

School activities

_____

_____

_____

_____

_____

Assessment of child and need for action (education, social, rules, happiness, and morals)

_____

_____

_____

_____

_____

_____

Decisions made during this semiyearly meeting

_____

_____

_____

# APPENDIX F

---

## Co-parent's Bill of Rights and Responsibilities

Developed by Frank Leek Ph.D.

1. To know where your child is.
2. To know whom your child is with.
3. To know when your child will be returned to you.
4. To know that your child is safe.
5. To know that your child is receiving structure and discipline in a positive and loving way.
6. To know you will be called immediately if your child is seriously injured or seriously ill.
7. To have appropriate telephone contact with your child when the child is with the other parent.
8. To have information about your children's activities when they are with the other parent.
9. To have current knowledge of school and extracurricular activities and a schedule of all meetings in which your children will receive awards and honors.

10. To receive realistic and useful information if your child is having a problem and be included in the process of change and improvement.
11. To know if your child is being seen by a therapist or counselor and have the responsibility to share in the cost and therapeutic activities.
12. To be appropriately involved in current and long-term planning of school and extracurricular activities, friendships, and relationships with family friends and relatives.
13. For you and your child to not be subjected to verbal, emotional, or physical abuse. To know that your child will not be spanked or physically punished by anyone other than the two primary parents and, if one parent is against corporal punishment, that neither parent will use such punishment.
14. To have your parenting plan honored by prompt and peaceful exchanges.
15. To preserve copyright to the titles "Mom" and "Dad."

# APPENDIX G

---

# A Child's Bill of Rights

Developed by the Wisconsin Supreme Court

Each child has the right to:

1. A continuing relationship with both parents.
2. To be treated not as a piece of property, but as a human being recognized to have unique feelings, ideas, and desires consistent with that of an individual.
3. Continuing care and proper guidance from each parent.
4. Not to be unduly influenced by either parent to view the other parent differently.
5. Express love, friendship, and respect for both parents: freedom from having to hide those stated emotions or made to be ashamed of such.
6. An explanation that the impending action of divorce was in no way caused by the child's actions.
7. Not to be the subject and/or source of any and all arguments.

8. Continuing, honest feedback with respect to the divorce process and its impact on the changing relationship of the family.
9. Maintain regular contact with both parents and a clear explanation for any change in plans and/or cancellations.
10. Enjoy a pleasurable relationship with both parents, never to be employed as a manipulative bargaining tool.

# APPENDIX H

Emergency Information

Mother _____     Father _____

_____             _____

Address _____     Address _____

_____             _____

Cell Phone _____  Cell Phone _____

_____             _____

Land Line _____   Land Line _____

_____             _____

Emergency Number _____    Emergency Number _____

_____             _____

Emergency Number _____    Emergency Number _____

_____             _____

Pediatrician _____ Telephone _____

_____ _____

Dentist _____ Telephone _____

_____ _____

School _____ Telephone _____

_____ _____

Day Care Provider _____ Telephone _____

_____ _____

Insurance Carrier _____ Telephone _____

_____ _____

_____

_____

_____

_____

_____

_____

_____

# APPENDIX I

---

## A Script for a Peaceful Exchange

*Mother and five-year-old daughter Bea drive up to Dad's house.*

**Mom:** Here we are. You get to see Dad now. Let's go knock on the door.

**Bea:** Okay. What if he is not there?

**Mom:** I think he is. If not, he will be here soon.

**Bea** (reaching door): I want to ring the doorbell.

**Mom:** Okay.

*Dad opens the door.*

**Dad:** Hi, Bea. Hi, Mom. Good to see you. Why don't you both come in?

*Bea is now making the inner transition, and normal behaviors will be slightly exaggerated. She is a reserved child, taking in information, processing it, and then talking. Now she is quiet as she speaks.*

**Bea:** Hi, Daddy.

**Mom:** She has been a great girl all week. I am sure she will want to show you her schoolwork. I am so proud of her.

**Dad:** I really want to see that.

**Mom:** It has been a really nice day today, hasn't it?

**Bea** (she has now made the inner transfer): Daddy, guess what? I brought my new teddy bear! Do you want to see her?

**Dad:** I sure do.

**Mom:** Well, you guys got a lot to talk about. Bea, I'll see you after dinner on Sunday.

*Bea tries to internalize the pain of missing Mom.*

**Bea:** Okay, Mommy.

**Mom:**  Give me a kiss bye.

**Bea:** Okay. [She kisses Mom.]

**Dad:** We will see you Sunday. Thanks for coming over.

*Mom leaves, suffers a whole lot, gets in her car, and goes to a prearranged place that is fun for her to dampen the pain.*

# APPENDIX J

---

# A Script for When Disaster Strikes

*Dad calls Mom for their weekly telephone call.*

**Dad:** I guess we really blew it when we were talking about vacations the other day, didn't we?

**Mom:** I didn't blow it. You were wrong.

**Dad:** Maybe. I think we need to talk about it.

**Mom** (thawing a bit): Yeah. I thought we were past stuff like that.

**Dad** (misusing humor): Well, I will retract the statement about you being a four-hundred-pound gorilla.

**Mom:** Yeah. [Long pause, recovering from misused humor.] And I guess you are not a relative of Attila the Hun. [Long pause regretting attempts at humor.] It seems like whenever we talk about vacations, we both get really angry. Even when we were together, we always fought about that.

**Dad:** Yeah. [Long pause.] Should we try to talk about vacations on our own, or do we need help?

**Mom:** Why don't we have a special thirty-minute telephone call to discuss our vacation plans? If that doesn't work, then we should have a mediator help us. But I have to work this through soon; at work they are putting a lot of pressure on us to sign up for the time we want.

**Dad:** Sounds good to me. I am getting the same kind of pressure. When can we talk about that? Tomorrow evening?

**Mom:** Yeah. How about 9:00 p.m.?

**Dad:** Good. Now let's finish our weekly telephone call.

# APPENDIX K

─────◈◈◈─────

# A Script for Attending the Same Activity

*Mom arrives with little Bobby at his first soccer game. Dad is already there with his new wife.*

**Mom:** Hi, George. Hi, Barbara. Nice day for a soccer game.

**Dad:** Hi, how are you?

**Barbara:** Looks like Bobby is all ready to play!

*Bobby runs over to Dad and Barbara.*

**Bobby:** Hi, Dad. Hi, Barbara. The coach said I could play today. Are you going to watch?

**Mom:** Why don't you all talk a minute? I'll find Bobby and me a seat. He is supposed to sit in the stands until his team goes out on the field.

*Mom walks away to find seats for her and Bobby.*

**Dad:** How you doing, Son?

**Bobby:** Great!

*Dad, Barbara, and Bobby talk for three or four minutes, and then Dad takes Bobby to where Mom is sitting.*

**Dad:** Here he is. We are really looking forward to seeing him play. Have a great game, Bobby.

*On the other side of the field, a fight breaks out between divorced parents who have not had the benefit of the excellent skills you have mastered.*

# An Interactive Book:
# A Request from the Author

Raising children in two homes is a recent change in our lifestyle. As recently as three generations ago, families stayed together, often living in the same house from birth to death. That has changed. We are now a mobile, changing society. In this book I have brought together what I know about this new way of raising children. Now I would like to hear from you. I would like to hear about your successes. Please select one of the twenty essential co-parenting tasks that you have mastered and tell us how you did it. If possible, I will use what you tell us in a book tentatively titled *Parents Speak from Beyond the Great Divide*. Your reward will be acknowledgment of what you have written, with your first name, initials, or, if you wish, your full name.

Frank Leek, Ph.D.
SPSP@comcast.net